Holger Schmidt

SAMProc

Holger Schmidt

SAMProc

A Middleware for Highly Dynamic and Heterogeneous Environments

Südwestdeutscher Verlag für Hochschulschriften

Impressum/Imprint (nur für Deutschland/ only for Germany)
Bibliografische Information der Deutschen Nationalbibliothek: Die Deutsche Nationalbibliothek verzeichnet diese Publikation in der Deutschen Nationalbibliografie; detaillierte bibliografische Daten sind im Internet über http://dnb.d-nb.de abrufbar.

Alle in diesem Buch genannten Marken und Produktnamen unterliegen warenzeichen-, marken- oder patentrechtlichem Schutz bzw. sind Warenzeichen oder eingetragene Warenzeichen der jeweiligen Inhaber. Die Wiedergabe von Marken, Produktnamen, Gebrauchsnamen, Handelsnamen, Warenbezeichnungen u.s.w. in diesem Werk berechtigt auch ohne besondere Kennzeichnung nicht zu der Annahme, dass solche Namen im Sinne der Warenzeichen- und Markenschutzgesetzgebung als frei zu betrachten wären und daher von jedermann benutzt werden dürften.

Verlag: Südwestdeutscher Verlag für Hochschulschriften Aktiengesellschaft & Co. KG
Dudweiler Landstr. 99, 66123 Saarbrücken, Deutschland
Telefon +49 681 37 20 271-1, Telefax +49 681 37 20 271-0
Email: info@svh-verlag.de
Zugl.: Ulm, Universität Ulm, Diss., 2009

Herstellung in Deutschland:
Schaltungsdienst Lange o.H.G., Berlin
Books on Demand GmbH, Norderstedt
Reha GmbH, Saarbrücken
Amazon Distribution GmbH, Leipzig
ISBN: 978-3-8381-1408-8

Imprint (only for USA, GB)
Bibliographic information published by the Deutsche Nationalbibliothek: The Deutsche Nationalbibliothek lists this publication in the Deutsche Nationalbibliografie; detailed bibliographic data are available in the Internet at http://dnb.d-nb.de.

Any brand names and product names mentioned in this book are subject to trademark, brand or patent protection and are trademarks or registered trademarks of their respective holders. The use of brand names, product names, common names, trade names, product descriptions etc. even without a particular marking in this works is in no way to be construed to mean that such names may be regarded as unrestricted in respect of trademark and brand protection legislation and could thus be used by anyone.

Publisher: Südwestdeutscher Verlag für Hochschulschriften Aktiengesellschaft & Co. KG
Dudweiler Landstr. 99, 66123 Saarbrücken, Germany
Phone +49 681 37 20 271-1, Fax +49 681 37 20 271-0
Email: info@svh-verlag.de

Printed in the U.S.A.
Printed in the U.K. by (see last page)
ISBN: 978-3-8381-1408-8

Copyright © 2010 by the author and Südwestdeutscher Verlag für Hochschulschriften Aktiengesellschaft & Co. KG and licensors
All rights reserved. Saarbrücken 2010

Table of Contents

Table of Contents   i

1 Introduction   1
    1.1 Problem Statement 3
    1.2 Main Contributions 3
       1.2.1 Architectural Design Pattern for Fundamentally Adaptive Applications . 4
       1.2.2 Infrastructure Support for Mobile and Ubiquitous Computing Scenarios . 5
       1.2.3 Model-driven Development of Fundamentally Adaptive Applications . . . 7
    1.3 Structure of this Thesis 8

2 Application Requirements in Mobile and Ubiquitous Computing Environments   11
    2.1 Mobile and Ubiquitous Computing 11
    2.2 Adaptive Applications in Mobile and Ubiquitous Computing Scenarios . . . 12
       2.2.1 Cyber Foraging – Distributed Ray Tracing 12
       2.2.2 Follow-me – Mobile Multimedia Player 14
       2.2.3 Crisis Management – Report Application 15
    2.3 Summary of Software Requirements 16

3 AXM: Architectural Design Pattern for Fundamentally Adaptive Applications   19
    3.1 Related Work 20
       3.1.1 Mobility 20
       3.1.2 Fundamental Adaptivity 23
       3.1.3 Summary 24
    3.2 AXM Architectural Design Pattern 27
       3.2.1 AXM in a Nutshell 27
       3.2.2 Fundamental Adaptivity 29
       3.2.3 Basic Entities and Collaboration 33
       3.2.4 Basic Security Considerations 34

Table of Contents

    3.3 AXM Prototypes 35
          3.3.1 AOM: Adaptive Object Migration 36
          3.3.2 AWSM: Adaptive Web Service Migration 43
    3.4 Case Studies: AXM for Adaptive Applications in Mobile and UbiComp Scenarios 50
          3.4.1 Cyber Foraging – Distributed Ray Tracing 50
          3.4.2 Follow-me – Mobile Multimedia Player 57
          3.4.3 Crisis Management – Report Application 59
    3.5 Summary 61

4 Infrastructure Services for Mobile and Ubiquitous Computing Environments 63
    4.1 Dynamic Management of Code 63
          4.1.1 Related Work 64
          4.1.2 Necessity of Non-functional Property Support 66
          4.1.3 Generic Infrastructure for Decentralised Dynamic Management of Platform-specific Code 69
          4.1.4 Dynamic Management of Platform-specific Code with OSGi 78
          4.1.5 Basic Security Considerations 86
    4.2 Generic Context Service 87
          4.2.1 Background 87
          4.2.2 Related Work 88
          4.2.3 Requirements 90
          4.2.4 Context Service 91
          4.2.5 Basic Security Considerations 95
          4.2.6 Integration of Context Support into AWSM 95
    4.3 Entity Discovery with the Session Initiation Protocol 98
          4.3.1 Session Initiation Protocol 99
          4.3.2 SIP Extension to support Entity Discovery 101
          4.3.3 Decentralised SIP with Extension to support Entity Discovery 106
          4.3.4 Performance Evaluation 111
    4.4 Soap*ME*: A Lightweight Java ME Web Service Container 115
          4.4.1 Related Work 116
          4.4.2 SoapME Requirements 118
          4.4.3 SoapME 118
          4.4.4 Service Development 124
          4.4.5 Evaluation 126
    4.5 Summary 128

5 Development Support — 131
5.1 Building Adaptive Applications with Self-adaptive Mobile Processes — 132
5.2 Self-Adaptive Mobile Process Execution Language — 134
5.2.1 Description Language — 135
5.2.2 Automatic Code Generation — 146
5.3 Modelling Self-Adaptive Mobile Processes — 152
5.4 Related Work — 154
5.5 Summary — 155

6 Conclusion — 157
6.1 Main Contributions — 158
6.2 Limitations and Future Work — 159

Bibliography — 163

List of Figures — 179

List of Abbreviations — 183

1
Introduction

Currently, we are approaching Mark Weiser's [Wei91] vision of ubiquitous computing (UbiComp). There, heterogeneous devices in the environment, such as cell phones, personal digital assistants (PDAs), sensors and desktop machines, build up spontaneous and dynamic networks. These devices provide a great potential of computing power, which should be used to assist users. For instance, these resources can be used for cyber foraging [Sat01], an approach in which resource-demanding calculations are swapped out from mobile devices to surrogates in the environment to save computing resources on the mobile devices. This certainly requires infrastructure support; especially support for heterogeneity is a severe issue. Due to the fact that applications are running within such a highly heterogeneous environment, they require being *fundamentally adaptive* in terms of providing fundamental mechanisms to change the application according to the current application context (e.g., characterised by platform, programming language and hardware). At the same time, novel applications in mobile scenarios, such as follow-me applications [TST01], demand for novel features, such as application migration (e.g., a mobile media player, which continuously uses the best multimedia output device in a mobile user's surroundings). Moreover, fundamental application adaptivity offers the opportunity to even actively adapt the application to use the environment to full capacity (e.g., to run computationally intensive parts of an application with native code by migrating the application to

1 Introduction

powerful devices in the surroundings). While being fundamentally adaptive, applications should remain addressable. This is essential for mobile and UbiComp systems for being able to foster collaboration between applications and can be implemented with a persistent unique application identity. However, it is a highly complex and thus error-prone task to develop applications, which are able to manage system dynamics and fundamental adaptivity in terms of dynamically changing and even migrating the application according to the respective application context.

The traditional approach of application developers to deal with heterogeneous environments is to implement distributed applications with distributed objects (e.g., CORBA objects [OMG04a]) or Web services [W3C04c]. These objects and services implement parts of the application logic and provide interfaces being remotely accessible to interact with each other in order to provide the overall application functionality. However, in mobile and UbiComp scenarios, applications face high system dynamics. There are applications, such as follow-me applications that require parts of the application functionality being available at the local device. Even if the required application logic is initially available, the situation can dynamically change (e.g., when a mobile user changes the network). Thus, standard distributed applications are not sufficient due to the fact that these have to be installed on the respective devices in advance. Additionally, they provide only a base technology to implement applications and the development of large-scale applications is still highly complex. These issues restrict the use of standard distributed applications in spontaneous environments.

An advanced data-centric approach is the use of workflow systems, such as proposed by *Satoh* [Sat05, Sat06]. There, a central workflow engine orchestrates the underlying stationary distributed objects or services on the basis of a workflow description that is provided by the application developer. This eases application development. On the basis of such systems, *Kunze et al.* [KZL06] introduce mobile workflows, i.e., workflows that are transferred between workflow engines at runtime. Although this is a promising approach to distribute the workflow execution, it leads to high resource consumption in general because it requires an engine for workflow interpretation on all participating devices. Especially in mobile and UbiComp environments this is not acceptable because of the resource-limited devices in use.

A more dynamic approach is the use of mobile code, i.e., mobile agent (MA) platforms supporting run-time migration from one machine to another one at runtime [FPV98] like *Aglets* [LO98]. This is especially useful in dynamic and spontaneous environments as the application does not have to be installed on all participating devices in advance (actually, such a pre-installation is impossible as already described before). Yet, in general, these MA systems require uniform execution environments regarding platform and programming language. Most rely on Java and use native serialisation [Sun05a] to implement migration. This turns them into an inappropriate candidate for heterogeneous environments. Especially mobile and UbiComp scenarios with embedded devices require support for resource-conservative native languages, such as C and C++. Solutions to this issue are MA systems supporting heterogeneity, such as *Agent Factory* [BOvSW02]. However, these systems still lack an overall solution for dynamic loading of unavailable code on demand and automatic state transfer (usually, both mechanisms have to be implemented manually). Moreover, there is no support for dynamic fundamental adaptation of the application at runtime (e.g., to fundamentally adapt an application by restricting its functionality on a resource-limited device), which is essential in mobile and UbiComp scenarios to get the most out of the available execution resources.

1.1 Problem Statement

This thesis addresses three important problems that arise in the context of mobile and UbiComp application development as described before.

- First of all, support for heterogeneity is insufficient in current infrastructures. If at all, migration between heterogeneous nodes is only possible with manual implementation of migration functionality in the application logic. Such an approach requires a deep understanding of the application and the infrastructure in use. Hence, application development is complex and error-prone.

- Secondly, current strategies to implement adaptation steps in an application are cumbersome and thus error-prone. Such systems with adaptation support require manual implementation of the adaptation steps. In general, this leads to strongly intermingled adaptation and application logic. Maintaining such kind of code is highly demanding.

- Thirdly, mobile and UbiComp applications have to be well-suited for resource-constrained devices. Having only little memory available does not allow having the entire code present on all potential target nodes for migration. Furthermore, it is often undesirable to have the fully-fledged functionality present on every node the application migrates.

1.2 Main Contributions

The following sections briefly introduce the main contributions of this thesis with respect to the aforementioned problems and relate them to the current state-of-the art. First of all, this thesis

1 Introduction

proposes a solution that faces the issue of heterogeneous migration with an abstract state description that is mapped to environment-specific representations and code for automatic conversion. Secondly, regarding the implementation of adaptive applications, this thesis proposes a solution that aims at supporting the developer by separating the adaptation from the application logic. The key goal is to integrate an abstract description for fundamentally adaptive applications. This approach results in enabling the use of model-driven development (MDD) techniques for generating the fundamental adaptation logic of these applications being able to run in heterogeneous mobile and UbiComp environments. Last, with respect to resource-constrained devices, this thesis presents a solution that minimises the memory utilisation by loading tailored code on demand and minimising the data necessary for execution.

1.2.1 Architectural Design Pattern for Fundamentally Adaptive Applications

Due to insufficient system support for applications being able to manage system dynamics and fundamental adaptivity, there is a high demand for an architectural design pattern supporting the development of such applications. This thesis introduces *adaptive x migration* (AXM), a novel architectural design pattern for fundamentally adaptive applications with two concrete implementations, i.e., adaptive Web service migration (AWSM) and adaptive object migration (AOM). Unlike related work, the pattern enables fundamental adaptation in terms of changing the application location at runtime (i.e., *weak migration*[1] [FPV98]) and by dynamically replacing parts of the provided functionality, available state and the implementation in use while maintaining a unique identity. The approach is generic in the sense that it has only very little demands on the underlying base infrastructure and can be mapped to common object- and service-based middleware infrastructures. More concrete, AXM only requires a method to map method calls, call parameters as well as data structures to different implementation languages, and support for communication references, application identity and application deployment at runtime. Actually, this is exactly what is provided by major middleware platforms, such as CORBA [OMG04a], Web services [W3C04c] and also .NET [Mic09]. This claim is proved by providing two AXM-based prototypes being implemented with CORBA objects (i.e., *AOM objects* [KSSH06]) and Web services (i.e., *AWSM services* [SKHR08]). Yet, the author advocates the use of Web services in mobile and UbiComp scenarios as these have already achieved acceptance in standard environments. This is supported by the fact that there is promising work on Web services providing reasonable communication between heterogeneous sensors [LKNZ08]. Moreover, this thesis presents novel applications calling for fundamental adaptivity that demonstrate the feasibility of the AXM approach.

---
[1]Only application state is transferred but no execution-dependent state, such as stack values and CPU registers.

1.2.2 Infrastructure Support for Mobile and Ubiquitous Computing Scenarios

Dynamic management of code is an essential part of application migration in a dynamic environment. There, challenges arise if rarely used code has to be loaded on demand or if code to load is not even known in advance. This is a common problem, as distributed applications usually have numerous independently running application parts. This results in some code not being known at compile time and even at start-up time. Yet, it is desirable that newly developed code can be used by already running execution environments. Additionally, for some applications it is not feasible to install and load all implementation code at every node of the system. For instance, some code might only be used by a few nodes and these nodes may not be known in advance or have resource restrictions.

For enabling migration to locations where the necessary code is locally unavailable, this thesis suggests a dynamic and decentralised code management service. This service allows peers to offer and to obtain platform-specific code on demand. The decentralised dynamic code management infrastructure is generic in the sense that it is independent of the peer-to-peer (P2P) infrastructure in use (only keyword search has to be supported). Alternatively, the developed infrastructure is able to integrate a centralised code management service for an improved resource usage on mobile devices due to the fact that there is no need for traffic to maintain the P2P infrastructure. In contrast to related work, such as *Java Web Start* [Sun05b] and the work of *Paal et al.* [PKF05], the proposed service allows centralised and decentralised dynamic discovery of implementation code and is not restricted to a particular programming language. Additionally, it provides means to automatically select appropriate, system-tailored implementations with respect to functional and non-functional properties. Thus, it excellently fits highly dynamic and heterogeneous scenarios. Moreover, this thesis shows a transparent integration of the dynamic code management service in OSGi [OSG07a] due to the fact that OSGi is a key-technology to support on-demand deployment of complex Java-based applications. Finally, it proposes a seamless adoption of the OSGi-based service within AWSM.

Mobile and UbiComp scenarios are characterised by high system dynamics due to the ad-hoc nature of device interconnection. Thus, most decisions of an application have to be made at runtime, such as if an application should be fundamentally adapted or which code should be loaded. This highly depends on the current application context (i.e., all information characterising the current situation of the application). Thus, applications have to be context-sensitive.

This thesis introduces a novel context service for mobile and UbiComp applications. For supporting the required heterogeneity the context service provides a Web service interface. It manages system dynamics by providing context management functionality, i.e., for collecting, discovering and monitoring of context at runtime. To represent the context, it builds on a novel generic context model with a modular architecture to support all kinds of applications. In contrast to related work, such as proposed by *Schmidt et al.* [SAT+99] and *Indulska et al.* [IRRH03], this eases integration of further context components (i.e., parts of the context building the overall context) and allows decentralised modelling of context using heterogeneous context sources. Additionally, the proposed service uses only standards for describing and querying context information. For describing the context it uses the Web Ontology Language (OWL) [W3C04a] and for discovery the powerful SPARQL Protocol and RDF Query Language (SPARQL) [W3C08].

A service for discovering entities, such as users, devices and services is a crucial part of dynamic mobile and UbiComp systems. In particular, if the mentioned context service is not available, such a service can be used as a lightweight alternative.

This thesis proposes an integration of entity discovery with the *Session Initiation Protocol* (SIP), a common coordination protocol for multimedia services. For instance, it is used for next generation networks [ITU04] as proposed by the *IP Multimedia Subsystem* (IMS) specification [3GP09] for upcoming mobile phone networks. With only small extensions on top of standard SIP, entities may be registered and searched for. Unlike state-of-the-art approaches, the approach omits the additional overhead of implementing separate entity discovery services. The solution is compliant to the SIP standard and offers the same level of flexibility as common entity discovery protocols. Yet, general problems with the standard SIP infrastructure, for instance in UbiComp ad-hoc networks, lead to a trend of integrating P2P mechanisms into SIP. This thesis proposes a novel architecture for decentralised SIP networks on the basis of JXTA [Gon01], which maintains compatibility with standard SIP. Unlike related approaches, various P2P algorithms can be integrated according to custom requirements and the architecture supports entity discovery. An evaluation of the P2P approach shows that it compares well to standard SIP in terms of response time but results in more traffic for maintaining the P2P overlay.

There are several Web service containers for standard Java to run the required infrastructure services, such as Apache Axis [Apa06]. Yet, these containers demand for powerful execution devices. Java Micro Edition (ME) provides a basic Java environment for mobile devices, such as PDAs and mobile phones. It requires only minimal resources and provides two configurations, i.e. the Connected Device Configuration (CDC) and the Connected Limited Device Configuration (CLDC). CDC is intended for powerful devices, whereas CLDC is also running on resource-limited devices.

This thesis presents Soap*ME*, a flexible and lightweight Web service container for Java ME. For supporting as many devices as possible Soap*ME* is based on CLDC because CLDC-compatible applications are also able to run in a CDC environment [Sun06a]. Having broad acceptance in the Web service community, SOAP [W3C07b] is used for Web service invocations. Soap*ME* provides high flexibility by supporting dynamic Web service deployment at runtime. Additionally, it offers several extension points, such as for invocation interception and for changing the transport protocol. Thus, Soap*ME* provides all required means to implement AWSM on top of it. There is no comparable Web service container for Java ME CLDC. There is only JME SOAP Server [Sou06a], a very rudimentary Java ME CLDC Web service container. In contrast to Soap*ME*, JME SOAP Server does not provide any extension points and does not support dynamic deployment at runtime. This thesis describes the Soap*ME* prototype implementation, which provides reasonable performance and compliance to the SOAP *test collection* specification [W3C07d].

1.2.3 Model-driven Development of Fundamentally Adaptive Applications

For supporting the development of fundamentally adaptive applications on the basis of *AWSM services* this thesis suggests a model-driven approach. Therefore, the concept of a self-adaptive mobile process (SAMProc) is introduced, which provides a novel abstraction for fundamentally adaptive applications. It allows the abstract specification of applications that are able to change their behaviour and location during lifetime. The basic idea is to describe the application as a SAMProc and to use this information to automatically generate the fundamental adaptation logic of an appropriate *AWSM service* in a model-driven process.

For describing a SAMProc this thesis presents a novel XML-based description language, i.e., the Self-adaptive Mobile Process Execution Language (SAMPEL). Due to the fact that the Business Process Execution Language (BPEL) already provides means for orchestration of *standard* Web services, SAMPEL is implemented as a BPEL extension, which additionally supports describing *AWSM service* behaviour with respect to fundamental adaptation in terms of location, functionality, state and implementation. This thesis presents a tool, which automatically generates the fundamental adaptation logic of the corresponding *AWSM service*. Thus, application developers have to implement the pure application logic only. In comparison to related work, such as proposed by *Ishikawa et al.* [ITYH06] and *DEMAC* [KZL06], the SAMProc approach is more lightweight because it generates code which is not interpreted but executed at runtime. Thus, there is no more need for evaluating the process description at runtime, which saves resources on the affected devices. Additionally, SAMProc allows dynamic, system-tailored application deployment at runtime. This supports devices with limited resources (e.g., storage, memory and

1 Introduction

CPU) as incoming (i.e., migrating) applications are automatically deployed, executed, migrated to another network node and thus undeployed again.

Additionally, this thesis introduces an Eclipse plug-in that allows describing fundamentally adaptive applications with a graphical notation. Modelling with the Eclipse plug-in results in an automatic generation of an appropriate SAMPEL description. Thus, in the overall process, this approach allows generating the fundamental adaptation logic of a fundamentally adaptive application with only few clicks.

1.3 Structure of this Thesis

This thesis is structured as follows. First, Chapter 2 discusses requirements for applications running in mobile and UbiComp environments. Therefore, this thesis introduces exemplary novel applications, which represent a broad set of adaptive distributed applications for mobile and UbiComp scenarios. These are a cyber foraging application (i.e., a distributed ray tracing application), a follow-me application (i.e., a mobile multimedia player) and a crisis management application (i.e., a mobile report application). Thereafter, the overall application requirements are defined on the basis of these application needs.

Chapter 3 introduces AXM, a novel architectural design pattern for fundamentally adaptive applications that meets these requirements. After an in-depth discussion of related work providing support for such applications, special attention is given to the fundamental adaptivity capabilities of AXM and the required network entities to implement the approach. Then, the chapter describes two prototypes implementing the AXM pattern: AOM on the basis of CORBA and AWSM on the basis of Web services (in each case with interoperable implementations for Java and C++). The end of the chapter presents the implementation and the respective performance of the exemplary applications of the previous chapter.

For assisting applications in mobile and UbiComp scenarios Chapter 4 provides advanced infrastructure services supporting dynamic and heterogeneous environments. After discussing the fundamental requirements of a service for dynamic loading of platform-specific code being unavailable at a particular location, the chapter shows the implementation of such a service on the basis of the P2P platform JXTA [Gon01]. This is followed by an integration of this service into the OSGi framework being a key-technology to support on-demand deployment of complex, modularised Java-based applications [OSG07a]. Special attention is given to the integration of the Java-based AWSM prototype with OSGi to show the feasibility of the approach. Then, after determining the requirements of a generic context service, the next part of the chapter introduces the context model and the architecture of such a service. Again, to show the feasibility of the approach, the service is integrated into the AWSM prototype and used for the implementation of the mobile multimedia player application of Chapter 2. The next part of the chapter proposes a novel SIP-based service for dynamically discovering entities, such as users, devices and services. After a brief introduction of SIP, the necessary SIP extension is described in detail. Then, a decentralised approach is presented and evaluated. The last part of the chapter is devoted to Soap*ME*. After defining the requirements for a lean Java-based Web service container, the Soap*ME* architecture is presented with special attention to dynamic deployment of Web services at runtime. Instructions on service development with Soap*ME* and a brief performance evaluation conclude the chapter.

Chapter 5 presents support for the development of fundamentally adaptive applications. First, the concept of SAMProc is introduced as an abstraction, which allows automatically generating implementation code of fundamentally adaptive applications on the basis of AXM in a model-driven manner. Therefore, the chapter describes the novel SAMPEL description language and shows an appropriate code generator for AWSM as feasibility study. Then, an Eclipse plug-in is presented that is able to generate an appropriate SAMPEL description from a graphical application model.

Finally, Chapter 6 concludes by highlighting the main contributions of this thesis and depicting their limitations. It discusses open problems and challenges for future work.

2

Application Requirements in Mobile and Ubiquitous Computing Environments

This chapter discusses requirements for applications in mobile and UbiComp environments. First, the following section briefly introduces the idea of mobile and UbiComp and describes the typical system characteristics. The subsequent section brings up three novel applications for such scenarios, which are used throughout the rest of this thesis. Finally, general software requirements are derived from the needs of these applications.

2.1 Mobile and Ubiquitous Computing

In the early nineties, *Mark Weiser* envisioned a future of *ubiquitous computing* (UbiComp), in which everyday life of people should be unnoticeably supported by small, mobile devices in the surroundings [Wei91]. These devices should be ubiquitous in the sense that people do not recognise them as computational devices anymore. According to Weiser, this evolution is comparable to the early 80ies when personal computers (PCs) superseded mainframes (at that time, mainframes were only used for special applications). The term *mobile computing* is similar to the idea of UbiComp. Yet, in mobile computing all devices are mobile but not essentially ubiquitous.

Currently, we are approaching Weiser's vision with an increasing number of small devices with computing power and network connectivity being available. Users already start using mobile devices, such as MP3 players, mobile phones, PDAs and laptops instead of standard PCs. These premises provide the ability to develop novel applications, such as a personal information manager that guides users through everyday life according to the current location. Due to more and more mature user interfaces, devices start disappearing as visible computational devices in terms of UbiComp.

From the author's point of view, mobile and UbiComp provide great prospects for future applications. Overall, there is a great potential of computing power in the surroundings as many people will take all kinds of computing devices with them. These devices can be interconnected and their computational power can be shared, which results in great cooperation possibilities among the participating devices and users. This potential calls for novel applications.

2.2 Adaptive Applications in Mobile and Ubiquitous Computing Scenarios

This section introduces three exemplary mobile and UbiComp scenarios: a cyber foraging, a follow-me and a crisis management application. Whereas the first two applications examine how an application on a mobile device can use external resources from a single-user perspective, the last one targets a more complex setting where multiple users try to solve a common goal (i.e., to document a large accident and coordinate rescue operations). As already motivated in the introduction, these scenarios call for fundamentally adaptive applications to use the environment to full potential. All applications are examined regarding their particular software requirements.

2.2.1 Cyber Foraging – Distributed Ray Tracing

The first application is a novel cyber foraging application [Sat01] implementing distributed ray tracing. The general idea is to effectively use complex ray tracing algorithms on powerful stationary devices while presenting the results on resource-limited mobile devices, such as PDAs and subnotebooks. A possible scenario is interactive ray tracing [WBS03] for a virtual reality application running on a mobile device.

2.2 Adaptive Applications in Mobile and Ubiquitous Computing Scenarios

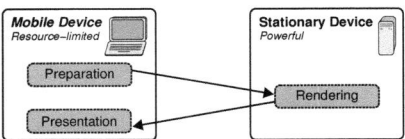

Figure 2.1: Basic workflow of ray tracing application

Such a ray tracing application is characterised by a basic workflow (see Figure 2.1). First, the scene is prepared by specifying the content and configuring the lights, then the scene is rendered, and finally the completed scene is presented within a graphical user interface (GUI). The preparation and the presentation steps can be processed on resource-limited mobile devices without difficulty. There, high-level languages, such as Java (i.e., standard and micro edition [Sun09a]) can be used, which eases GUI development. By contrast, the rendering step should be executed on a powerful device. Additionally, for reducing the execution time the rendering step requires using more efficient programming languages, such as C and C++. For displaying the overall progress the application should be able to monitor the rendering process.

Moreover, if the mobile device is connected to the Internet it should be able to offload the rendering to a more powerful machine (e.g., inside a cloud computing infrastructure [VRMCL09]). If the Internet is not accessible a quality reduced, less resource-intensive rendering process should be performed on the node itself. Especially for the latter, multiple implementations are necessary as the rendering-process has to be optimised for the executing hardware and due to the high variety of operating systems and programming languages for mobile devices.

As already motivated in the introduction, this thesis advocates using fundamental adaptation with support for migration to implement the ray tracing application. Thus, the workflow of ray tracing can be seen as an application that is migrated for using the environment to full potential (i.e., to migrate to the most powerful devices in the surroundings for rendering the scene). Due to the fact that such an application is not a standard application and to support dynamic changes in the availability of powerful devices, dynamic code loading is required if the code is unavailable on the particular device. Furthermore, such an application requires fundamental adaptivity in terms of programming language (e.g., Java vs. C and C++) and functionality (each step in the application workflow needs different functionality). While being fundamentally adaptive (especially in terms of migration), there is a need for permanent addressability because it should be possible to monitor the state of the application for its whole lifetime.

2 Application Requirements in Mobile and Ubiquitous Computing Environments

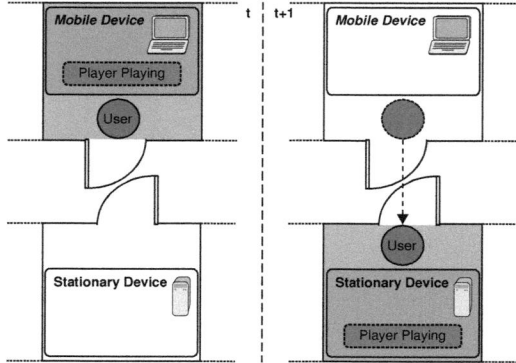

Figure 2.2: Basic workflow of mobile multimedia player

2.2.2 Follow-me – Mobile Multimedia Player

The second application is a novel mobile media player, which is implemented as a follow-me application [TST01]. The media player is mobile to allow using the best presentation device in the surroundings. This supports scenarios, such as the following: a user plays video on her mobile device and arrives at home; there, the application automatically recognises superior output devices in the surroundings and the presentation switches over to a bigger TV screen (see Figure 2.2). Thus, in contrast to the first example, not only compute-intensive tasks are off-loaded but hardware resources in the proximity of the user are used for an improved user experience.

The mobile media player application consists of two parts: a presentation component, which is controlled by a remote control component. Both components are implemented as independently migratable applications. This allows, for instance, keeping the remote control on the mobile device while migrating the presentation component on a stationary device displaying the media on a TV screen.

In addition to requiring dynamic deployment to allow migrating to all supporting devices in the surroundings, the application needs fundamental adaptivity. This refers to fundamental adaptivity in terms of implementation (due to the heterogeneous environment with different hardware running different programming languages and platforms, such as media presentation

2.2 Adaptive Applications in Mobile and Ubiquitous Computing Scenarios

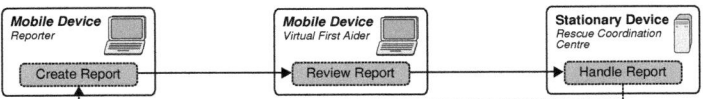

Figure 2.3: Basic workflow of report application

using the Java Media Framework (JMF) [Sun02] vs. the Mobile Media API (MMAPI) [Sun06e]) and functionality (e.g., only audio or video on particular devices with only one output facility). Finally, the approach requires addressability to allow the remote control connecting to the presentation component independent from its current location and implementation in use.

2.2.3 Crisis Management – Report Application

The third application is a novel application supporting crisis management by providing means for people in the crisis surroundings to document the current situation. Such a documentation system is able to support rescue coordination centres to provide emergency services with up-to-date information about the scene. Additionally, such a documentation system can help afterwards with the investigation of causalities. For instance, at the crash of a Concorde airplane near Charles-de-Gaulle airport in the year 2000 the cause could be clarified afterwards due to private recordings. Another example for the power of spontaneous reporters is the crash of a US Airways airplane plunging into the Hudson River in 2009. There, information about the scene spread faster via Twitter than via traditional media [Mar09].

In such crisis situations, people in the scene surroundings (i.e., *spontaneous reporters*) with mobile hardware (e.g., a cell phone, a PDA or an Internet tablet) should be able to initiate a basic report workflow to document the current situation for the *rescue coordination centre* (see Figure 2.3). Therefore, these spontaneous reporters enter text, audio and video messages into a report application on the mobile device. The code, which is required for this application, is initially provided by the rescue coordination centre (e.g., using the multimedia messaging service [Sev99] it is possible to send the application to all mobile devices that are connected to mobile networks, such as UMTS and GSM, in the scene surroundings). After successfully entering the documentation, the report is sent to *virtual first-aiders*. These are particular persons in the scene area, which undertake the task of reviewing the report: they verify the information and reject meaningless reports to disburden the rescue coordination centre. Only important reports are forwarded to the rescue coordination centre where the reported data is presented in order to act accordingly. Additionally, rescue coordination centres are able to initiate subsequent mobile report workflows to ask for further information from distinguished reporters.

Like the ray tracing application, this thesis advocates implementing the report application on the basis of fundamental adaptation with support for migration (see Chapter 1). With respect to this, unique reports can be seen as self-contained applications, which are migrated to implement the mobile workflow. Again, this requires dynamic deployment on demand to support the dynamic environment and to allow migration to all possible devices in the surroundings. Additionally, the application requires fundamental adaptivity in terms of programming language (due to the heterogeneous environment with different hardware), functionality (each step of the mobile workflow needs different functionality) and state (e.g., anonymous reviewing: information about reporter should not be available at the virtual first-aiders but at the rescue coordination centre). The mobile report should be addressable for its whole lifetime for reporters being able to monitor what happened to their report.

2.3 Summary of Software Requirements

The presented applications sketch a broad set of different mobile and UbiComp scenarios. The following paragraphs give an overall summary of their requirements.

All the presented applications require some form of *fundamental adaptivity*. They need a flexible concept to dynamically change the application behaviour (i.e., functionality to implement a basic mobile workflow), runtime (i.e., implementation to support heterogeneity) and footprint (e.g., minimal state, implementation and functionality to support resource-limited devices). Furthermore, applications are required to be *migratable*. Through this, they are able to benefit from specific context in the surroundings (e.g., users, computing power, provided services and connected devices). In contrast to a data-centric approach, in which only data is transferred, on the one hand, such an approach calls for dynamic application deployment and undeployment on demand, which is definitely not a trivial issue. On the other hand, migration has the great potential to free resource-limited devices from preinstalling all possible applications in advance. Actually, this is even impossible due to the fact that the presented applications are not standard applications and all possible devices cannot be determined in advance because of the dynamic environment. Dynamic deployment allows migrating to devices, where the necessary code is not known in advance, which supports the dynamic nature of the example scenarios.

Regarding migration it is also important to *support heterogeneity* of the surrounding devices. Due to the fact that each connected device in the surroundings is potentially able to contribute, there is highly heterogeneous hardware, such as laptops, PDAs, mobile phones and even sensors. In general, for executing applications such devices are further characterised by offering different operating systems, programming languages and platforms.

In addition to providing fundamental adaptation support for device-tailored applications, the infrastructure services themselves should be resource-conservative according to the respective device capabilities. This results from the fact that embedded hardware within the physical devices may be limited (e.g., memory, CPU, energy). Thus, mobile and UbiComp infrastructures have to pay special attention to *support resource-limited devices*.

While being fundamentally adaptive, applications still have to be *permanently addressable* to allow for cooperation and monitoring. This requires an application identity, which remains constant for the whole application lifetime. A mobile and UbiComp infrastructure should even allow the localisation of participating objects in the surroundings in general. This could be supported by a discovery process mechanism for objects on the basis of either metadata (e.g., type and location) or the respective object identifier. For eventually interacting with one another, applications require *communication*. Due to the fact that participating devices are characterised by heterogeneity, interoperability is needed. Therefore, common standards for application-to-application communication, such as Web services, should be used.

Mobile and UbiComp scenarios are characterised by high system dynamics. This results from the fact that more and more computing power is embedded into everyday objects. In conjunction with network connectivity these objects are able to spontaneously build up open networks. Additionally, as devices are mobile, some of them might not be reachable anymore, whereas new devices can be discovered. For a prompt reaction to such system changes, a dynamic notion of *context* is needed within the applications and the infrastructure. This comprises context about the current execution environment of the application (e.g., current resource usage and location) as well as about other execution environments (e.g., current load and provided services). Due to high system heterogeneity, context metadata has to be standardised to ensure the interoperability among applications and infrastructure services in the surroundings.

As a result of the diverse set of requirements, application development for mobile and UbiComp scenarios is a highly complex and thus error prone task. Thus, for making these requirements controllable, there should be *development support*, for instance on the basis of a model-driven approach. Ideally, there should be automatic code generation support using high-level abstractions for enabling application development being independent from the underlying infrastructure in use. This would allow application developers focusing on the mere application logic.

3
AXM: Architectural Design Pattern for Fundamentally Adaptive Applications

This chapter introduces *adaptive x migration* (AXM), a novel architectural design pattern for fundamentally adaptive distributed applications that meets the requirements defined in Chapter 2. AXM supports fundamental adaptation in terms of dynamically changing the location (i.e., weak application migration), provided functionality, available state and the implementation in use. Prior to describing the AXM approach in detail, this thesis explicitly discusses related work regarding fundamentally adaptive and in particular mobile applications (i.e., in terms of supporting migration). Then, the chapter highlights the fundamental adaptivity capabilities of AXM and the required network entities to implement the approach.

For showing the generality of the approach, this chapter shows two prototypes implementing the AXM pattern: AOM on the basis of the Common Object Request Broker Architecture (CORBA) and AWSM on the basis of Web services. Both prototypes are implemented with interoperable implementations for Java and C++ without any changes regarding the respective middleware platform in use. This chapter concludes by showing the AXM-based design and the implementation of the exemplary applications of the previous chapter with their respective performance in a typical mobile and UbiComp setting.

3 AXM: Architectural Design Pattern for Fundamentally Adaptive Applications

3.1 Related Work

This section provides a comprehensive overview on related work regarding fundamentally adaptive and in particular mobile applications. Thereby, the section focuses on systems that practically support at least one aspect of fundamental adaptivity as well as on more abstract proposals such as specifications. This is inline with the generality of the architectural design pattern and the two concrete prototypes on the basis of the pattern. After giving details on the particular systems in the respective sections, a summary compares these systems with each other according to their common main aspects.

3.1.1 Mobility

Application mobility is essential to tackle dynamic environments. The following paragraphs present details on system support for applications being implemented as mobile objects, services and agents. Live migration on the basis of virtual machines (e.g., *Clark et al.* [CFH[+]05]) is not considered due to the fact that these systems only allow migrating virtual machines as a whole; AXM offers a much more fine-grained migratability in terms of applications. Additionally, virtual machine migration is restricted to a homogeneous environment regarding the hypervisor.

3.1.1.1 Mobile Objects and Services

There is a vast number of systems supporting application mobility in terms of objects and services. For instance, there are several approaches providing programming language support for object migration. Already in 1988, the *Emerald* [JLHB88] programming language provided strong object migration in homogeneous environments (i.e., regarding hardware architecture). Later, in 1995, *Steensgaard and Jul* [SJ95] presented an extended approach for strong object and thread migration in heterogeneous environments on the basis of Emerald. They implemented heterogeneous migration by automatically converting the execution state, such as program counters, into a machine-independent format. Nevertheless, this approach is restricted to the Emerald programming language and thus is not acceptable for heterogeneous environments with devices supporting different programming languages.

In addition to programming language support, there is also system support for mobile objects. For instance, *Garbinato et al.* introduce frugal objects (FROBs) for mobile and pervasive computing [GGH[+]05, GGH[+]07]. FROBs implement an event-based computing model, in which FROBs provide fundamental adaptivity in terms of their interface (i.e., accepted events) and code. FROBs support weak object migration but require a novel programming model, which does not allow standard statements, such as loops and forks.

Peter and Guyennet [PG00] provide a generic solution for heterogeneous CORBA object migration based on the CORBA Life Cycle Service (LCS) specification [OMG02]. They require describing the object state as an IDL structure, which is used to generate special objects carrying the mobile object state. Thus, the developer has to manually externalise and internalise the mobile object state. Additionally, *Peter and Guyennet* do not address concepts for fundamental adaptation of the mobile object. Previous work [KSH05] co-authored by the author of this thesis presents another approach for weak object migration on the basis of the CORBA LCS specification. In contrast to *Peter and Guyennet*, it uses CORBA value types (i.e., objects with call-by-copy semantics) to implement mobile objects. Due to the fact that value types are implicitly transferred as a copy to the target location (as parameters of a remote method), developers do not have to care about externalisation and internalisation of the mobile object.

In addition to systems supporting object migration, there are also approaches for implementing application migration on the basis of service migration. For instance, *Hammerschmidt and Linnemann* [HL06] present stateful Web service migration. For implementing service migration they build on Java serialisation. Thus, this approach is limited to Java, which is insufficient in mobile and UbiComp environments. Additionally, system dynamics are not well supported as the target location for migration is statically specified.

3.1.1.2 Mobile Agents

In the past, a lot of mobile agent (MA) systems were developed. An MA is a special kind of mobile application, which acts autonomously and is able to migrate for fulfilling its task. Most of these systems allow weak migration but only in homogeneous environments due to the fact that they rely on native Java serialisation. Examples for such MA systems are *MOA* [MLC98], *Mole* [SBH97, BHRS98] and *Aglets* [LO98]. Additionally, there are also MA systems supporting strong migration, such as *D'Agents* [GCK+02]. Nevertheless, strong migration in the *D'Agents* system is restricted to Tcl and Java and does not provide means for agent migration in heterogeneous environments.

Takashio et al. [TST01] propose an MA framework to implement follow-me applications. Their system provides MAs with means to adapt their code to the current context. Thus, applications are able to benefit from using high-performance implementations on powerful devices. Nevertheless, the solution requires a Java runtime environment and therefore does not support heterogeneous environments. Furthermore, *Ishikawa et al.* [IYTH04] describe an MA system for Web service integration in UbiComp environments. In their approach MAs implement basic workflows: MAs are able to move to particular locations in order to obtain efficient local access to Web services. However, their approach is also restricted to Java as it uses native Java serialisation to implement migration.

There are MA systems for heterogeneous environments as well, such as *Agent Factory* [BOvSW02]. There, the authors propose a platform-neutral approach for weak agent migration. Instead of transferring the MA code, only a blueprint is transferred. Such an approach can be realised by assuming that an MA consists of a set of components. These are composed on the basis of the transferred blueprint at the migration target location by a special *Agent Factory*. However, the approach still lacks a solution for dynamic loading of unavailable code and automatic state transfer.

Choy et al. [CBM99] conceptually developed a CORBA environment for MAs on the basis of mobile CORBA objects. Therefore, they used the CORBA LCS but apparently the concept has never been implemented. Additionally, the *Secure and Open Mobile Agent* (SOMA) programming framework for MAs was introduced by *Bellavista et al.* [BCS00]. SOMA is compliant to CORBA and the MA standards MASIF [MBB+99] and FIPA [ON98]. Thus, it is compatible with other MA systems. Like Agent Factory, all mentioned systems lack dynamic loading of unavailable code and automatic state transfer.

There are also more high-level approaches for application mobility. For instance, *Binder et al.* present an architecture for ad-hoc processes [BCF+06] being executed by MAs. Their MAs contain an XML process description for necessary local invocations. This leads to a dynamic itinerary for the MAs but the architecture is restricted to Java. Another system is the *Distributed Environment for Mobility-aware Computing* (DEMAC) [KZL06] targeting the distributed execution of processes. Therefore, a custom process description language was developed. Instead of migrating the application, only process descriptions are transferred for providing some kind of mobility. Thus, the DEMAC approach is similar to mobile workflow management systems, such as proposed by Satoh [Sat05, Sat06]. However, these systems require a process execution engine on all participating devices, which conflicts with supporting dynamic mobile and UbiComp environments with all kind of devices (e.g., resource-limited devices).

To sum it up, most of the presented mobile object and MA systems provide only migration support for homogeneous Java environments using native Java serialisation. There are only some systems for heterogeneous environments on the basis of CORBA. Moreover, a very crucial requirement in mobile and UbiComp environments is support for fundamental adaptation to the current runtime context. Besides the work on FROBs, there is no mentioned system providing flexible fundamental adaptation of an MA's and mobile object's state, functionality and implementation at runtime. Only CORBA-based approaches (e.g., *Bellavista et al.*), *Takashio et al.* and *Agent Factory* provide limited fundamental adaptation support of the MA's and mobile object's implementation at migration time. Thus, the following section presents a broad overview of systems supporting fundamentally adaptive applications.

3.1.2 Fundamental Adaptivity

There are different approaches to achieve fundamental adaptivity of applications. First of all, there is programming language support. For instance, the *Self* programming language [SU95] allows manipulation of an object's methods and state at runtime on the basis of the *prototype concept* [NTM01]. There, an application developer is able to copy existent objects and to dynamically modify the behaviour according to the current need instead of using inheritance for specialisation. Due to the limitations of *Self* as a local programming language, there is also *dSelf*, a distributed Self variant [TK02]. Another programming language with respect to fundamental adaptivity is *AmbientTalk* [DvCM+05] building on the ambient-oriented programming (AmOP) paradigm. *AmbientTalk* tackles volatile connections as well as system dynamics with an active object model on the basis of concurrent distributed prototypes. Although *dSelf* and *AmbientTalk* are promising approaches, there is no support for heterogeneous object migration with support for heterogeneous programming languages.

In addition to programming language support, there are also systems that are built on the basis of the *tuple space* paradigm [Gel85]. There, application data is shared as tuples in a distributed system. For instance, *Limbo* [DWFB97] was the first tuple-space–based platform supporting adaptive applications in mobile environments. Yet, tuple spaces require a special programming model and do not support dynamic fundamental adaptation of application functionality and implementation at runtime.

There is also middleware support for fundamentally adaptive applications. For instance, *Almeida et al.* introduce a dynamic reconfiguration service for CORBA [AWvSN01]. The proposed service is able to upgrade applications in terms of objects at runtime. Objects do not have to be taken offline by entailing operations for migration, replacement, addition and removal. In contrast to the AXM pattern, the dynamic reconfiguration service does not allow replacing the object interface and state at runtime. Furthermore, another drawback is that developers have to manually implement methods for state introspection and modification.

An MA-based approach to fundamental application adaptation was proposed by *Mendez and Mendes* with the *Agent Transport Service* (ATS) [MM99]. They considered the CORBA LCS but in order to support lightweight agents it was discarded: in contrast to all migration methods being offered by the MA itself these methods are entirely provided by the ATS. Unlike the AXM approach, ATS does not provide support for fundamental adaptation of the MA state and functionality. Another MA system for implementing fundamentally adaptive applications was introduced by *Brandt et al.* [BHR01, BR00]. Their MAs are reassembled from small subcomponents. This allows exchanging context-dependent implementation parts at runtime. This is comparable to the AXM prototypes, which also provide means for loading context-specific implementations at runtime on the basis of *dynamic code management* (DCM) (see Section 4.1). In contrast to AXM, *Brandt et al.* do not provide means to change the application interface at runtime according to the current context.

Furthermore, there are component-based [Szy02] middleware platforms to implement fundamentally adaptive applications. For instance, *PCOM* [BHSR04] focuses on the development of a distributed component-based system, which allows dynamic adaptation of component dependencies at runtime. Thus, parts of the application implementation can be reconfigured at runtime (in terms of components). Internally, *PCOM* builds on the *BASE* middleware [BSGR03], which provides abstractions to access remote services transparently. A similar approach on the basis of distributed components is the *Mobility and Adaptation Enabling Middleware* (MADAM) [AEHS06]. There are also Web-service–based middleware platforms for fundamental application adaptation on the basis of component-like reconfiguration. For instance, *Erradi et al.* introduce *Manageable and Adaptive Service Compositions* (MASC), a policy-based middleware for adaptive composite Web services [ETM07]. There, applications are dynamically composed of different Web services (implementing parts of the application). In contrast to reconfiguring parts of the application, the AXM approach propagates replacing the application (e.g., Web service or CORBA object) with a fundamentally adapted one. Thus, AXM allows optimal resource usage by fundamentally adapting the application to a device-tailored one (e.g., in environments with resource-limited devices). Nevertheless, Web service composition can be used in conjunction with the AXM implementation for Web services, for instance, to integrate legacy services

3.1.3 Summary

After an in-depth discussion of related work, the following paragraphs compare the features of the related systems with the AXM approach according to important mobile and UbiComp requirements, such as heterogeneity, mobility, adaptivity and communication.

Due to the fact that mobile and UbiComp scenarios are generally built upon open systems with quite a number of different devices, support for heterogeneity is a severe issue. Figure 3.1

3.1 Related Work

Project Name	Heterogeneity			Mobility		Adaptivity		
	Language	Platform	Hardware	Strong	Weak	Code	Functionality	State
AgentFactory	+	+	+	−	+	−	−	−
Almeida et al.	+	+	+	−	+	+	−	−
AmbientTalk	−	−	+	−	−	−	+	+
ATS	+	+	+	−	+	−	−	−
Binder et al.	−	+	+	−	+	−	−	−
Brandt et al.	−	+	+	−	+	+	−	+
Choy et al.	+	+	+	−	+	+	−	−
D'Agents	+	+	+	+	−	−	−	−
DEMAC	−	−	−	−	+	−	−	−
dSelf	−	−	+	−	−	−	+	+
Emerald	−	−	−	+	−	−	−	−
Emerald extension	−	−	+	+	−	+	−	−
FROBs	−	+	+	−	+	+	+	+
Hammerschmidt et al.	−	+	+	−	+	−	−	−
Ishikawa et al.	−	+	+	−	+	−	−	−
Kapitza et al.	+	+	+	−	+	+	−	−
Limbo	+	+	+	−	−	−	−	+
MADAM	−	+	+	−	−	+	+	+
MASC	+	+	+	−	−	+	+	+
MOA, Mole, Aglets	−	+	+	−	+	+	−	−
PCOM	−	+	+	−	−	+	+	+
Peter and Guyennet	+	+	+	−	+	+	−	−
Satoh	−	+	+	−	+	−	−	−
Self	−	−	+	−	−	−	+	+
SOMA	+	+	+	−	+	−	−	−
Takashio et al.	−	+	+	−	+	+	−	−
AXM	**+**	**+**	**+**	**−**	**+**	**+**	**+**	**+**

Figure 3.1: Related approaches: support for heterogeneity, mobility and fundamental adaptivity

provides details on heterogeneity support in related work, such as language, platform and hardware heterogeneity. There are some systems supporting all these kinds of heterogeneity, such as *D'Agents*, *AgentFactory*, *ATS* and *SOMA*. However, AXM is the only approach that goes even one step further by providing an architectural design pattern with an abstraction for technologies, such as Web services and CORBA objects.

Furthermore, this thesis advocates that application mobility is the key to an improved usage of resources in the surroundings in a mobile and UbiComp environment. Figure 3.1 also lists the

3 AXM: Architectural Design Pattern for Fundamentally Adaptive Applications

Project Name	RPC	Messages	Events
AgentFactory	+	−	−
Almeida et al.	+	−	+
AmbientTalk	−	+	−
ATS	+	−	−
Binder et al.	+	+	−
Brandt et al.	+	−	+
Choy et al.	+	−	−
D'Agents	−	+	−
DEMAC	+	−	−
dSelf	+	−	−
Emerald	+	−	−
Emerald extension	+	−	−
FROBs	−	−	+
Hammerschmidt et al.	+	+	−
Ishikawa et al.	+	+	−
Kapitza et al.	+	−	−
Limbo	−	−	−
MADAM	+	−	−
MASC	+	+	−
MOA, Mole, Aglets	−	+	−
PCOM	+	−	−
Peter and Guyennet	+	−	−
Satoh	−	+	−
Self	−	−	−
SOMA	−	+	−
Takashio et al.	−	−	+
AXM	**+**	**+**	**(+)**

Figure 3.2: Related approaches: support for communication types

capabilities (i.e., weak vs. strong mobility) of related work in comparison to the AXM approach. There are some systems supporting strong mobility, such as *Emerald* and *D'Agents*, but they require a completely homogeneous environment regarding language and platform. There are also systems that overcome the issue of heterogeneity with weak mobility, such as provided by *Almeida et al.* and Peter and Guyennet. Yet, the AXM approach with its prototypes for CORBA and Web services is the only one that supports weak mobility in heterogeneous environments without requiring developers to implement any basic migration support themselves.

In addition, fundamental adaptivity is essential to adapt the application to the application context (e.g., tailored application on resource-limited devices vs. fully-fledged application on powerful devices; see Section 2.2.1). Figure 3.1 provides details on related work capabilities with respect to adaptivity. Only *FROBs* and component-based approaches, such as *PCOM*, provide fundamental application adaptivity regarding code, functionality and state. Yet, the AXM approach with its prototypes is the only one that provides complete fundamental adaptivity in heterogeneous environments without requiring the developer to implement the adaptation code.

Finally, for supporting a high number of applications, it should be possible to use any type of communication according to the particular application needs. Figure 3.2 shows related work with respect to RPC-, message- and event-based communication. There is no system that provides all types of communication so far. Yet, due to the fact that AXM is an architectural design pattern, it allows any type of communication. The current prototypes support RPC- and message-based communication. An event-based prototype has not yet been implemented but is possible as well.

3.2 AXM Architectural Design Pattern

This section presents the architectural AXM design pattern with a novel facet concept providing an abstraction for fundamentally adaptive applications. It introduces the core idea in a nutshell, shows fundamental adaptivity capabilities of the pattern and describes the necessary entities and their collaboration in an abstract manner. The last part presents basic security considerations.

3.2.1 AXM in a Nutshell

This thesis introduces a novel *abstract facet* concept for making applications fundamentally adaptive. It provides an abstraction from the fundamental adaptation steps of an application and can be seen as a particular role of an application. These abstract facets are implemented by a set of (concrete) facets. For instance, in the distributed ray tracing scenario of Section 2.2.1, there would be a respective facet representing the preparation, rendering and presentation steps. Such an application facet runs on a particular network *node* and comprises a particular *interface*, *implementation* and *state*.

An application implementation already determines the implemented interface, comprised state and the compatible nodes; specific nodes already determine executable application implementations. Thus, abstract facets can only comprise a particular interface and state and concrete

3 AXM: Architectural Design Pattern for Fundamentally Adaptive Applications

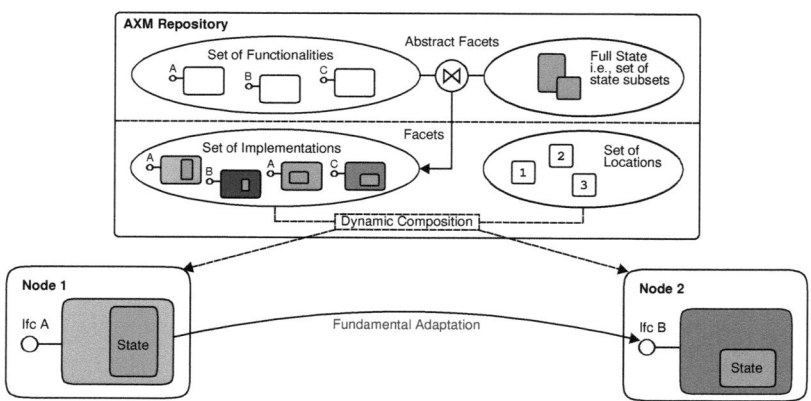

Figure 3.3: AXM facet concept: fundamental adaptation leads to dynamic composition of particular state, functionality, implementation and location while maintaining a unique application identity

facets can implement all possible combinations of interfaces and state with a particular implementation running on specific nodes. Such a design allows the developer to specify fundamental application adaptation in terms of abstract facets. Then, the AXM system is able to dynamically decide on which concrete facet to use. For this purpose, a concrete AXM implementation should provide an infrastructure entity, which is able to map abstract facets to appropriate concrete facets.

Figure 3.3 shows the overall schema of the AXM concept. All possible facets of an application are stored in the *AXM repository*. The available implementations and the corresponding nodes on which the implementations are executable represent the actual fundamental adaptation configurations of an application. These configurations build the fundamental adaptation basis and can be dynamically applied to an application facet at runtime by changing the application's location, interface, implementation and state (see Figure 3.4). Therefore, application developers have to specify the desired target facet directly in the source code. This can either be abstract or concrete facets. Yet, it is also possible to support developers by generating this implementation code from an abstract application model, such as proposed in Chapter 5.

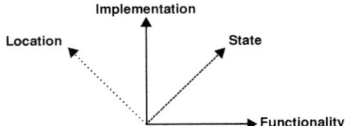

Figure 3.4: AXM supports dynamic fundamental application adaptation with respect to the four orthogonal axes location, functionality, implementation and state at runtime

Figure 3.3 illustrates an exemplary fundamental adaptation of an application by migrating from one node to another one with an adaptation of its facet with respect to the interface, implementation and state in use. Yet, a fundamental adaptation of single parts of the application facet is possible as well, such as changing only the location, interface, implementation or state. Yet, there has to be an appropriate target facet within the AXM repository. For instance, one could migrate an application from a resource-restricted Java environment to a powerful C++ environment. This requires only a fundamental adaptation of implementation and location.

A unique application identity, which allows addressing the application for its whole life time, is permanently maintained while fundamentally adapting the application. This is required for continuously addressing the application independent of its current facet with respect to the interface and location.

The following section further elaborates on the fundamental adaptivity feature of AXM.

3.2.2 Fundamental Adaptivity

AXM provides a very flexible fundamental adaptation mechanism in terms of dynamically changing and even migrating an application according to the respective application context.

3.2.2.1 Mobility

For achieving application mobility in terms of weak migration an appropriate target location has to be discovered. In order to interact with such target locations there have to be entities, which act as a representative to create the applications on the remote targets. For initiating the migration an appropriate contact address of such an entity has to be discovered by the migrating application. The address is either known by the application or a particular network entity is used, which is aware of possible target locations (see Section 3.2.3).

To create the application at the target location the necessary code has to be available there. Dynamic loading of code on demand allows migration even to locations where the required code is not available in advance. This is especially important in dynamic mobile and UbiComp environments where it is impossible to distribute the required code on all possible locations in advance. More details on dynamic loading of code within the AXM system are presented in Section 3.2.2.2.

After successful creation of the application at the target location, its state has to be transferred to restore the prior behaviour. A severe issue is ensuring consistent state at this stage. A basic approach is to block and delay requests for the application at the middleware level during migration time and to wait until all running requests are processed. After successful transfer of state, delayed requests are forwarded to the new location.

State exchange requires an interoperable state transfer format. In general, mobile object and MA systems use language-dependent features, such as Java serialisation. This is applicable in many standard scenarios but in mobile and UbiComp scenarios a solution with support for heterogeneity at code level is essential.

Before exchanging state, it has to be determined, which state to transfer. Yet, it is not reasonable to transfer the whole application state as the implementation can be replaced during migration (see Section 3.2.2.2). Thus, not all parts of the state might be interpretable by another implementation. AXM distinguishes *implementation-dependent state*, i.e., the complete state of a particular implementation, from *implementation-independent state*, representing the state of an application being interpretable by all possible implementations of a particular functionality. For instance, in case of a hash table implementation, implementation-independent state comprises the key-value pairs, whereas implementation-dependent state consists of variables being used for calculating the hash function. To sum up, AXM considers

- *Implementation-dependent state* as values that are specific for a certain implementation variant of an interface, and
- *Implementation-independent state* as values that are needed by any possible implementation to provide the functionality defined by an interface and values that would be considered as information loss if they were omitted.

Actual state variables of the particular implementation have to be mapped to the exchanged state in order to initially set the state of the application implementation (i.e., internalisation).

3.2 AXM Architectural Design Pattern

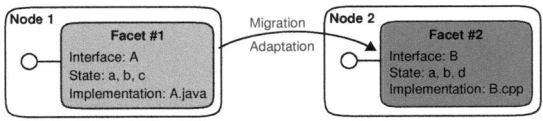

Figure 3.5: AXM facet concept: fundamental adaptation from one application facet into another one

The AXM pattern allows arbitrary mechanisms. For instance, in Section 3.3.2, a basic name matching algorithm is used to implement such a relationship (see Figure 3.5): If a facet #1 contains state variables with name a and b, state variables a and b within another facet #2 are considered the same. Thus, after fundamental adaptation from facet #1 into facet #2, variables a and b of facet #2 have to be set to the prior values of a and b within facet #1. The developer has to ensure that variable types are compatible; otherwise deserialisation results in an error. This is a common requirement for data exchange between services and in the context of distributed-object–based systems. Nonetheless, if larger and very complex scenarios are targeted more advanced approaches might be suitable (e.g., tagging state with semantic annotations on the basis of an ontology).

It is essential that the unique application identifier is maintained during migration. This enables transparent addressing of the application, for instance using a basic forward mechanism (see Section 3.3.1.6 and Section 3.3.2.6).

3.2.2.2 Dynamic Adaptation of Implementation

AXM provides means to replace the current application implementation on demand. This allows loading of node-tailored code according to functional and non-functional requirements. AXM assumes that the interface of an implementation determines its basic functional properties that can easily be checked against the functional requirements. This is a common feasible approach of many standard middleware platforms considering interfaces as contracts between client and server, such as CORBA [OMG04a] and Java RMI [Sun06d]. If the required code is already available at the location, it can easily be instantiated. If it is unavailable, dynamic loading of code is needed.

Dynamic loading of code requires dedicated infrastructure support by a code description repository that hosts the necessary information about available implementations and their individual properties. Furthermore, a code repository is needed, which basically stores and provides implementation code. The code description repository provides a query interface to the AXM infrastructure to find suitable implementations and to select the most appropriate one. Once the best-fitting candidate has been identified, it is loaded using the code repository. Section 4.1 introduces an infrastructure that meets these requirements.

To ensure stateful adaptation of the implementation at runtime the state has to be transferred during the fundamental adaptation as well (see Section 3.2.2.1).

3.2.2.3 Dynamic Adaptation of State

In addition to dynamic adaptation of the implementation at runtime, AXM provides a mechanism to adapt the current application state (i.e., implementation variables in use). In general, this implies using a different implementation as well as different variables. Thus, a core task of state adaptation is state exchange between different implementations as described in Section 3.2.2.1.

As an abstraction for the adaptation of state, AXM partitions the application state into *active state* and *passive state*. AXM defines active and passive state as follows:

- *Active state* is represented by the state variables that are used and needed for fulfilling the functionality of the application within a certain facet.

- *Passive state* is the state of an application that is not needed, not available or not accessible within a certain facet.

Passive state has to be stored to allow later reuse within another facet (see Section 3.2.3). There, for instance, the basic name matching algorithm for state internalisation as presented in Section 3.2.2.1 could be used.

3.2.2.4 Dynamic Adaptation of Functionality

As already mentioned in Section 3.2.1, AXM supports dynamic adaptation of the application functionality as well. This allows high flexibility of an application by dynamically providing a different set of available functionality (i.e., available interfaces; see Figure 3.3). Whenever needed, the required functionality is selected from the AXM repository and the appropriate implementation code and state is loaded.

3.2 AXM Architectural Design Pattern

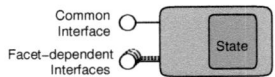

Figure 3.6: Common and facet-dependent interfaces of an AXM application

Although the approach provides a very flexible fundamental adaptation mechanism, the use of such flexible applications by clients (fundamentally adapting anything but the unique identifier) is difficult without reasonable conventions. Thus, AXM defines that each facet of a particular application *should* have a common facet-independent interface to ensure uniform access independent of the current facet interface (see Figure 3.6). For instance, such a common interface might have a method for obtaining the current application facet in use.

3.2.3 Basic Entities and Collaboration

Figure 3.7 shows the basic required entities and their collaboration to implement fundamental adaptation of an application with the AXM design pattern.

In the first step, the active state is stored in a *state store* entity, which can either be located locally or remote with respect to the source application facet. The task of the state store is to passivate the application state for later use (i.e., state that can be activated within another facet again). This can arbitrarily be realised, for instance on the basis of an XML serialisation to a file. The state of the source facet has to be externalised and transferred to the state store according to Section 3.2.2.1.

Then, the target location is determined using a *factory finder* entity (i.e., fundamental application adaptation regarding location), which represents an abstract location following the model of the CORBA Life Cycle Service specification [OMG02]. It can be located on the same or a remote node relative to the source application facet and returns an appropriate *factory* entity, which is able to create applications on (remote) nodes. Therefore, the factory finder needs some kind of repository of available factories. This repository can be implemented arbitrarily, for instance with a static configuration file or with factories registering their current contact address, creatable application facets and context at the factory finder at runtime. To support the selection process, the source application facet specifies the requirements (e.g., concrete facet and context) for the target facet as a parameter of the search method of the factory finder. The factory finder is able to match the requirements with the available factories within its repository.

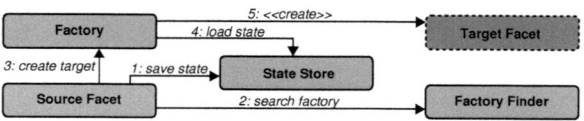

Figure 3.7: Collaboration of logical entities for AXM

Then, the factory creates the desired target facet with the needed active state of the respective facet (i.e., fundamental application adaptation with respect to functionality, implementation and state), which is loaded from the state store according to Section 3.2.2.1. In a last step, the application facet is started at the target location and the old facet is removed from the old location. Section 3.3 provides more details on real systems implementing this approach.

3.2.4 Basic Security Considerations

The following mechanisms provide basic security for the presented AXM pattern. Yet, only information security with respect to confidentiality and integrity is considered. Ensuring availability goes beyond the scope of this thesis. Though, standard mechanisms, such as replication could be used in general.

For allowing an application to rely on the platform there has to be a basic trust relationship between several entities. For instance, the process of selecting potential migration targets has to be secured. Due to the fact that application context is directly provided by the nodes, the factory finder and the factory have to establish a trust relationship with each other. Otherwise, malicious nodes are able to provide wrong context, which is then used by the factory finder for decisions about possible migration targets (on the basis of the given context requirements of an application; see Section 3.2.3). Moreover, malicious nodes are able to interfere with the selection process and thus can dramatically reduce performance.

For the same reasons, there has to be a trust relationship between the application and the factory finder. Otherwise, malicious nodes acting as a factory finder could manipulate the factory selection process.

Furthermore, there has to be a trust relationship between the application and the factory. Such a trust relationship is able to restrict migration to trusted factories (only if the application is able to verify the target factory). Under other circumstances, applications would be able to migrate to malicious nodes that are able to manipulate or terminate the application. Additionally, such a trust relationship allows factories to ensure that applications are only deployed if they are trusted. If not, malicious applications could have local system access with user privileges.

Furthermore, the state store has to reject malicious nodes, which try to override passive state. Thus, the method for saving state has to be secured by ensuring trust between the writing application and the state store. However, to ensure confidentiality by restricting data access from unauthorised entities, the loading method should be secured in the same way.

The issue of trust can basically be implemented with centralised or decentralised infrastructures. The *public key infrastructure* (PKI) [FS03] is a centralised approach on the basis of X.509 certificates [CSF+08]. There, certificate authorities are able to sign certificates and entities are configured to trust certificate authorities and their respective signed certificates. Furthermore, *Web of trust* is a decentralised approach, which is for instance used by *OpenPGP* [CDF+07]. There, *each* entity is able to sign certificates and entities are configured to trust *entities* (instead of certificate authorities) and their respective signed certificates. Yet, although these basic trust mechanisms can in general be used in mobile and UbiComp scenarios, there are also tailored approaches, such as proposed by *Lagesse* [Lag09]. Confidentiality and integrity can be ensured with encrypted communication (e.g., using the *Secure Sockets Layer* (SSL)).

In a basic approach, necessary certificates are installed on the respective entities' devices and whenever an application is created, an appropriate certificate is generated. This certificate should automatically be signed by an appropriate entity (i.e., certificate authority or trusted entity). Whenever an application is migrated, the certificate has to be passed with the invocation at the factory (see Section 3.2.3). Due to the fact that it can be ensured that the factory is a trusted entity, this is not a security issue if a secure, encrypted data transfer is guaranteed.

Section 3.2.2.2 propagates dynamic code deployment. Yet, dynamic code deployment enables malicious code injection. This issue can basically be solved with standard mechanisms, such as by introducing digital certificates for code [Nec97] and by using sandboxing mechanisms [WLAG93] for fine-grained restriction of system access. Though, Section 4.1.5 provides more details on security with respect to dynamic code deployment.

3.3 AXM Prototypes

For proving the claim that the AXM pattern can be implemented as a thin layer on top of common middleware infrastructures for heterogeneous systems, two prototypes were realised as part of this thesis: one for CORBA and another one for Web services. Both systems rely on an implementation-language–independent state description without any changes regarding the respective middleware (i.e., IDL for CORBA and WSDL for Web services). The following sections present the essential details to implement these prototypes. This should serve as some kind of recipe and thus ease porting the AXM pattern to other programming languages in addition to the currently supported ones (i.e., Java and C++).

3.3.1 AOM: Adaptive Object Migration

This section provides details on the CORBA-based prototypes to implement the AXM design pattern. There are two interoperable implementations for fundamentally adaptive objects (i.e., *AOM objects*): in Java, *AOM objects* run with the JacORB [The07b] and the Sun ORB (which is part of Java); in C++, they run with the Orbacus [Pro08]. Both prototypes are compliant to the AXM design pattern. The following section gives a brief introduction to CORBA and its Life Cycle Service (LCS) specification. Then, essential implementation details of the prototypes are presented.

3.3.1.1 Platform: CORBA

The *Common Object Request Broker Architecture* (CORBA) [OMG04a] is a middleware standardised by the Object Management Group (OMG). It allows developers creating and accessing objects in a distributed system while providing platform and language transparency to implement applications. Common middleware tasks, such as object location, request marshalling and message transmission are performed by the *Object Request Broker* (ORB). A remote object is specified by describing its interface using the *Interface Definition Language* (IDL). This interface is used to generate platform-specific *stubs* and *skeletons*, which act as surrogates dealing with heterogeneity and transparency (i.e., they handle remote invocations and marshalling for the object and its clients). Objects are implemented by *servants* that have to be registered at an *object adapter*. A client needs a valid object reference that can be bound by the local ORB instance to invoke remote methods.

The OMG specifies several CORBA services, such as the *Life Cycle Service* (LCS) specification [OMG02], which allows an application to control the distribution of objects (i.e., creating, removing, copying, and moving of objects). This introduces mobility and is especially useful for mobile applications and for the management of applications that need to distribute objects across different platforms for non-functional reasons, such as scalability and fault-tolerance.

The LCS assumes that object creation is performed using *factory* objects. These can also be remote, allowing for remote object creation. A factory is a CORBA object offering a method for creating new instances of a particular object type at a particular location. It is not specified how factories are requested to create a new object. This is left to the object developer as there can be different parameters required for different object types. However, the LCS specification defines an IDL interface named `GenericFactory`. This interface contains a generic `create_object()` operation, which gets a set of criteria that are represented as a sequence of name-value pairs. The LCS specification gives hints on how to use criteria but does not define any standards. For a specific factory implementation they can be used to select the required object type, object capabilities, different object initialisations, and even different locations.

While LCS object creation is handled by a factory, all other life-cycle operations are executed at the object itself. Therefore, an object supporting the LCS has to implement the `LifeCycleObject` interface. The `copy()` operation creates a copy of the object at some location. As a result, a reference to the newly created object is returned. The `move()` operation moves the object to another location and the `remove()` operation deletes the object. Both `copy()` and `move()` need some notion of location in order to place a copy or the object itself. The LCS specifies a `FactoryFinder` interface for objects representing an abstract location.

The CORBA LCS is just a specification. Although the interfaces are specified in detail, the flow of control is just roughly described and implementation details are left to the object developer and the service provider. On the one side, this allows for individual implementations of the specified interfaces, as the LCS specification deliberately underspecified certain issues in order to get them solved by an actual implementation. On the other side, it is likely that LCS implementations become system-dependent and incompatible. As a result of this, the author proposed a platform-independent implementation of the CORBA LCS specification [KSH05]. Yet, the LCS does not provide any means for dynamic fundamental adaptation of a mobile object according to the AXM design pattern.

3.3.1.2 Implementation Entities

Figure 3.8 shows the involved AOM implementation entities to fundamentally adapt a CORBA object on the basis of the AXM design pattern. To provide fundamental adaptivity, *AOM objects* have to implement the `AOMObject` interface, which defines the required life-cycle methods regarding fundamental adaptation[1]. The `AOMObject` is implemented as an activated value type (i.e., a special CORBA object providing call-by-value semantics) for enabling automatic programming-language–independent introspection of implementation-independent state (see Section 3.3.1.4). In addition to the proposed entities to implement the AXM pattern (see Section 3.2.3), the

---

[1] Regarding migration support, the AOM prototype is compliant to the CORBA LCS specification.

3 AXM: Architectural Design Pattern for Fundamentally Adaptive Applications

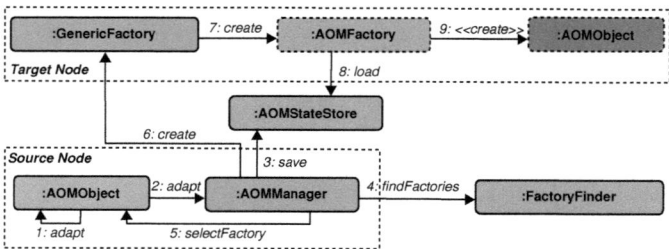

Figure 3.8: Collaboration of implementation entities for AOM

actual life-cycle operations are delegated to the *local* CORBA object AOMManager. For instance, in order to fundamentally adapt an *AOM object*, adapt() is delegated to the AOMManager (see Figure 3.8, Step 2), which manages the remaining steps for fundamental adaptation. A generic (i.e., application-independent) AOMManager is provided by the AOM prototype. For a custom application-specific factory selection process the AOMManager offers a call-back mechanism by calling selectFactory() at the *AOM object* (Step 5). There, appropriate factories are given as a parameter and selectFactory() (which is implemented by the application developer) has to return the desired one. The FactoryFinder is implemented as specified in the CORBA LCS specification. It is able to search for factories matching given criteria (e.g., name of facet to create and the needed context). Therefore, factories are able to register themselves with their supported criteria. Moreover, the conceptual factory, proposed in Section 3.2.3, is split into two entities. A GenericFactory—as specified in the CORBA LCS specification—provides a generic interface for object creation. It delegates creation requests to a specific AOMFactory (Step 7). This delegation mechanism is essential for the integration of dynamic loading of unavailable code (see Section 3.3.1.5).

3.3.1.3 Coordination

During fundamental adaptation, access to an *AOM object* has to be coordinated and restricted to ensure a consistent state that can be serialised and transferred to the target location. Thus, operations with respect to fundamental adaptation need exclusive access to the *AOM object* in the sense that all earlier invocations have terminated and all others are blocked until the operation has finished. The implementation of a custom coordination mechanism at object level

3.3 AXM Prototypes

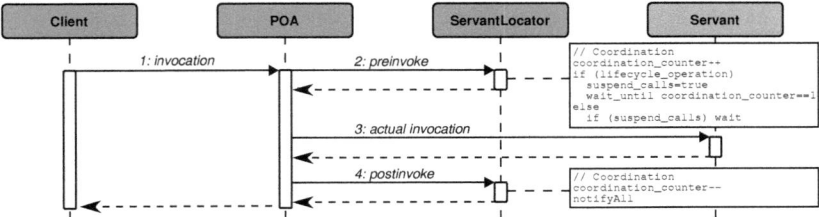

Figure 3.9: Coordination of concurrent invocations in AOM (with pseudo code)

can ensure this but requires a deep understanding of application functionality and thus is error-prone. Therefore, this thesis proposes a solution that is transparent to the developer of an *AOM object* on the basis of a standard CORBA *servant locator*.

A servant locator is responsible for activating and managing servants (see Figure 3.9). In general, it is used for servant management in conjunction with a database. For each incoming call the `preinvoke()` method of the servant locator is called by the Portable Object Adapter (POA). Then, the servant locator has to locate or set up an appropriate servant and return it to the calling POA. After the actual method invocation at the servant, the `postinvoke()` method of the servant locator is called to do management tasks (e.g., tear down the servant again).

For access coordination, the AOM prototype implements a servant locator encapsulating the access management on behalf of *AOM objects*. Each *AOM object* is registered at the locator on creation and has an invocation counter, which is increased for each incoming request (inside `preinvoke()`) and decreased when the corresponding response is sent (inside `postinvoke()`). This mechanism counts all running requests (see Figure 3.9).

A fundamental adaptation request can be detected by the servant locator because the name of the method to invoke is passed to the `preinvoke()` method. In case of running invocations, the request is suspended until all other invocations have finished[2]. Then, the invocation can be executed. Meanwhile, incoming invocations are suspended until the fundamental adaptation operation has finished. Then, in case of migration, these invocations are forwarded to the new location (see Section 3.3.1.6).

---

[2]Long-running application requests could be a bottleneck but they are rather uncommon in typical mobile and UbiComp scenarios.

3.3.1.4 State Transfer

Prior to transferring the state, it has to be determined. With CORBA value types implementing the *AOM objects* (see Section 3.3.1.2), developers are able to specify the state of a CORBA object. This state is the implementation-independent state due to the fact that a value type specification should be independent of the actual implementation. For obtaining the state information of a specific *AOM object* (i.e., the names of the implementation-independent state variables of a value type) in a platform-independent manner at runtime the `AOMManager` uses the standardised CORBA interface repository. Then, for actually reading the implementation-independent state, introspection is used. For the Java prototype, native Java reflection is used; for the C++ prototype, a special IDL compiler is provided, which generates methods for state introspection. With respect to further prototypes, there either has to be such a special IDL compiler for any CORBA-supported programming language that is not capable of native introspection, or developers have to implement the introspection methods on their own.

The implementation-independent *AOM object* state is transferred to the `AOMStore`. There, the state is stored and loaded with respect to the object identifier. Two methods for loading and saving the state are provided, which take the object identifier, the names and the values of implementation-independent state variables of the respective value type as parameters. The state values are passed as CORBA `Any` types. This way, heterogeneous mobile and UbiComp environments are implicitly supported by using the interoperable CORBA Common Data Representation (CDR) as transfer format for `Any` types.

In order to set the state, the interface repository is used again for determining the active state. Internalisation is implemented on the basis of Java reflection or generated C++ methods of the IDL compiler.

3.3.1.5 Dynamic Loading of Code

In dynamic environments, it is often required to transfer not only the state of an *AOM object* but also the implementation code if it is unavailable at the target location. It is possible to use the `code base` parameter of value types to dynamically load code on demand (as proposed in the CORBA specification). However, the specification defines that this code base directly references the code of one or more implementations, which is sufficient if a value type is copied between homogeneous environments but restricts flexibility if the value type is moved between different language environments. Additionally, in the AOM system there might also be missing

3.3 AXM Prototypes

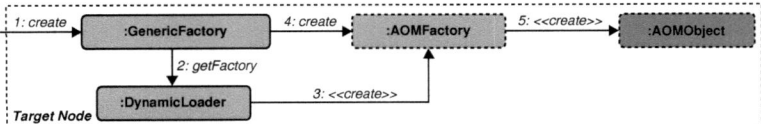

Figure 3.10: Dynamic loading of code with AOM

POA tie classes, which are not part of the value type code, but also have to be available for activating the value type.

Due to the restrictions of current dynamic code loading systems with respect to heterogeneous environments (e.g., [Sun05b, PKF05]), a more sophisticated approach was developed as part of this thesis supporting heterogeneous environments in an ORB-independent fashion. The novel *dynamic code management* (DCM) solution uses either a centralised [KH03] or a decentralised [KSBH07] repository, in which code as well as code descriptions are stored (see Section 3.2.2.2). For dynamic loading, the repository is queried for code fulfilling given functional and non-functional requirements. These requirements are compared to the properties of available code in the code description repository and then the best-fitting code is loaded from a code repository. More details about DCM with an elaborate discussion of related work can be found in Section 4.1.

Due to the above mentioned issues of the standard code-base mechanism of value types, the AOM prototype provides a `GenericFactory` on the basis of DCM (see Section 3.2.2.2). Figure 3.10 shows the integration of DCM. If `create()` is invoked and the necessary implementation code to create a new *AOM object* facet is unavailable at the target location, the DCM dynamic loader is invoked via the `getFactory()` method (see Figure 3.10, Step 1–2). As a parameter, the object *key* conforming to the interoperable CORBA *naming specification* [OMG04b] is passed. This key determines a concrete *AOM object* facet to load. If DCM is able to discover an appropriate platform-compatible facet in the code description repository, it loads the needed code from the respective code repository and instantiates a specific factory (Step 3), which implements the `AOMFactory` interface that is able to create the required *AOM object* facet. In case of Java, instantiating the specific factory is implemented with native reflection (i.e., using `Class.forName()` [Sun09d]); in case of C++, DCM uses standard *dlopen* mechanisms. Finally, the initial `create()` request is delegated by the `GenericFactory` to create the desired *AOM object* facet (Step 4 and 5).

3.3.1.6 Identity and Addressing

For uniquely identifying a fundamentally adaptive application, AOM uses the CORBA object identifier. For client-side transparency, the reference to an *AOM object* should be valid for its entire lifetime even after fundamental adaptation. In addition to a basic forwarder-based approach, where the servant locators at previous locations cooperate in locating *AOM objects*, the AOM prototype provides a location-service–based approach, where such a service tracks the current *AOM object* location [KSH05].

Inside the life-cycle methods the factory returns a reference pointing to the new location of the *AOM object*. This new location is implicitly announced by the AOM platform to the servant locator (i.e., a special `location` field of the *AOM object* is set, which can be read at `postinvoke()`; see Figure 3.9). This location value is registered in a global forwarding table. It is used to forward waiting calls that are resumed after migration (see Section 3.3.1.3) and all subsequent calls to the new location by throwing a standard CORBA forwarding exception. The client-side ORB transparently handles this exception by reissuing the request to the new location. Further requests are automatically forwarded to the new location as the ORB automatically caches location changes. This is a very simple approach with almost no additional overhead (only the forwarding table has to be maintained). However, it requires that the object adapters at previous locations stay up until the *AOM object* is finally removed and thus this method fails if only one of the hosts in the chain crashes or is down for some reason.

For avoiding those drawbacks the AOM prototype implements a *location service* as an additional solution. The key idea is to replace the *AOM object* references provided by the factory implementations in such a manner that they refer to a location service. Thus, invocations to *AOM objects* are initially sent to such a location service, which is then able to forward the invocation to the current location. For this task, the location service provides a CORBA management interface for registering and updating the current location of *AOM objects*. The location service itself is implemented as a servant manager, which throws a forward exception referring to the current location of the particular *AOM object*. It is important to note that every *AOM object* can have its own location service for reasons of load balancing.

According to Section 3.2.2.4, all facets of an *AOM object* should implement a common facet-independent interface for client-transparency of fundamental adaptation.

```
1  public abstract class AOMObjectImpl implements AOMObject {
2    public void preAdaptation(){...}
3    public void postAdaptation(){...}
4    public String adapt(NVP[] criteria, FactoryFinder there){...}
5    public String copy(NVP[] criteria, FactoryFinder there){...}
6    public String move(NVP[] criteria, FactoryFinder there){...}
7    public void remove(){...}
8  }
```

Figure 3.11: Abstract `AOMObjectImpl` class (Java)

3.3.1.7 Development Support

For supporting the developer, AOM provides an abstract `AOMObjectImpl` class for Java (see Figure 3.11). It contains generic code for introspection (see Section 3.3.1.4) and fundamental adaptation. Developers should inherit from this class to implement an *AOM object*. Through this, developers only have to implement the pure application and fundamental adaptation logic and to ensure state consistency among different facets (see Section 3.2.2.1).

The C++ prototype provides basic tool support. Due to the missing reflection support in C++, it provides a special IDL compiler, which generates C++ methods for state introspection. Additionally the implementation provides generic fundamental adaptation code as part of a shared object file, which can be used by developers.

3.3.2 AWSM: Adaptive Web Service Migration

This section introduces details on the AXM-based prototypes using Web service technology. The author developed an implementation for fundamentally adaptive Web services (i.e., *AWSM services*) on the basis of Apache Axis [Apa06] using Java and an interoperable implementation on the basis of gSOAP [EG02] with C++. The following sections briefly introduce Web services and show the essential implementation details of both prototypes (analogous to Section 3.3.1).

3.3.2.1 Platform: Web Services

Web services are a wide-spread XML-based application-to-application communication technology [W3C04c]. They are built upon standard Internet protocols and follow the service-oriented architecture (SOA) approach, in which functionality is provided only by services [SN96, Sch96].

Such services have an interface, a standardised service description and are addressed using standard communication protocols. Additionally, services can be composed of other services to build up complete applications.

Web services are uniquely identified by Uniform Resource Identifiers (URIs). They allow asynchronous document-based communication as well as remote method invocation. Service interface and protocol bindings are specified using the *Web Services Description Language* (WSDL) [W3C07e]. In WSDL, the interface is bound to a particular message protocol that is used for accessing the Web service. Common Web services use the message-based *SOAP* [W3C07b] protocol, a transport-protocol–independent XML application.

By building on XML, Web services are independent of platform and programming language. This allows their use in a heterogeneous environment. Dynamic environments are supported as well, as discovery and binding of Web services are handled at run-time. The *Universal Description, Discovery and Integration* (UDDI) [OAS04], a SOAP-based service, offers a generic interface to XML-metadata–based Web service discovery within a specific domain.

In contrast to CORBA, there is no specification for service migration, such as the CORBA LCS (see Section 3.3.1.1). Addressing of fundamentally adaptive services is also not covered by any specification and thus requires special treatment (see Section 3.3.2.6). Moreover, once implemented for a specific Web service container, service code is not inherently portable to other containers. Thus, dynamic loading of code is indispensable to load container-dependent code on demand (see Section 3.3.2.5).

3.3.2.2 Implementation Entities

Figure 3.12 shows the AWSM implementation entities and their collaboration to fundamentally adapt an *AWSM service* from one node to another. *AWSM services* implement the `AWSMService` interface, which provides life-cycle methods with respect to fundamental adaptation. In addition to the generic AXM concept in Section 3.2.3 (see Figure 3.7), the *AWSM service* uses a generic service-internal `AWSMManager` entity, which manages the whole adaptation on behalf of the *AWSM service* (see Figure 3.12, Step 2). The `AWSMManager` entity is provided by the AWSM prototype and is generic in the sense that it can be used by any *AWSM service*. For allowing a customised factory discovery process, a call-back mechanism is used to select the best-fitting factory out of the list of appropriate factories returned from the factory finder (see Figure 3.12, Step 5). Due to the available and standardised UDDI discovery mechanism for Web services, the `AWSMFactoryFinder` is implemented as a UDDI extension. It is able to search for factories satisfying given `criteria` (e.g., name of facet to create and the needed context). Furthermore,

3.3 AXM Prototypes

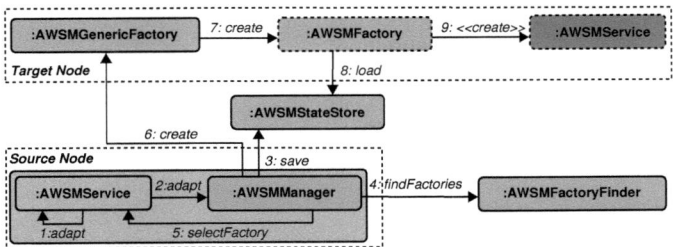

Figure 3.12: Collaboration of implementation entities for AWSM

in contrast to the generic approach in Figure 3.7, the conceptual factory is split into two implementation entities: a generic AWSMGenericFactory and a specific AWSMFactory, which is able to deploy a particular *AWSM service* facet (see Figure 3.12). This is essential to allow dynamic loading of code at runtime (more details can be found in Section 3.3.2.5).

3.3.2.3 Coordination

Before starting the fundamental adaptation when receiving an adapt() request, the AWSM system coordinates incoming and currently running requests. AWSM ensures that the incoming adapt() request is the only running request in order to establish a consistent state transfer (see Section 3.3.1.3).

The Axis-based prototype implements the coordination of requests with a request interceptor. Therefore, the abstract class BasicHandler[3] is extended, which is provided by Axis. If the interceptor is registered at the Axis container, a generic invoke() method is called, whenever an incoming request arrives at the container. As a parameter, a generic MessageContext object is passed from the container, which contains the service name and method to invoke. This is essential to intercept *AWSM services* only; standard Web services running within the same Axis container are not affected by this coordination feature. For this purpose, a global list contains all *AWSM services*, which have to be coordinated. For each *AWSM service*, there is an invocation counter, which is increased for each incoming request and decreased when the corresponding response is sent. When an incoming adapt() request is intercepted, the corresponding *AWSM service* is marked as adapting within the global list. This results in the adapt() request and all

---
[3] http://ws.apache.org/axis/java/apiDocs/org/apache/axis/handlers/BasicHandler.html

```
 1  <wsdl:definitions xmlns:wsdl="...">
 2    <wsdl:types>...</wsdl:types>
 3    <wsdl:portType name="MyPortType">
 4      <wsdl:operation name="getX"> ...
 5      </wsdl:operation>
 6    <wsdl:service name="MyService">
 7      <wsdl:port>...</wsdl:port>
 8      <awsm:states xmlns:awsm="...">
 9        <state type="xsd:string" name="x" />
10        <state type="xsd:int" name="y" /> ...
11      </awsm:states>
12    </wsdl:service>
13  </wsdl:definitions>
```

Figure 3.13: WSDL description with implementation-independent state

further requests being delayed within a queue until all currently running requests are finished (i.e., when the number of running requests is equal 0). Then, the `adapt()` request is unblocked. When the `adapt()` response is sent successfully, all prior blocked requests are forwarded to the new location (see Section 3.3.2.6).

The gSOAP approach works analogously. There, an *AWSM-service*-specific `process_request()` method (part of the actual *AWSM service* implementation), which is responsible for serving SOAP requests, implements the server-side interceptor for coordination on the basis of an invocation counter.

Both approaches intercept external invocations only. Thus, it is important to note that developers have to ensure state consistency themselves in the case of application-internal invocations.

3.3.2.4 State Transfer

As already mentioned in Section 3.2.2.1, the application state has to be transferred to restore the prior behaviour of the *AWSM service* at the target node. Therefore, an interoperable state transfer format has to be defined. To support heterogeneous environments it has to be language-, platform- and hardware-independent. This thesis proposes using XML schema data types [W3C04d] for transferring state from/to the `AWSMStateStore` due to the fact that these are used within standard SOAP messages, which fulfil the needed conditions of interoperability.

Prior to transferring the state it has to be determined (i.e., externalisation). Java provides native reflection for externalising the complete state of an object but only implementation-independent state has to be transferred (see Section 3.2.2.1). Due to the fact that implementation-independent state cannot be determined automatically [KSH05], the Axis prototype uses Java annotations (`@ImplementationIndependentState`) to let developers mark implementation-independent state. For mapping the Java state type to the corresponding transfer format type, a standard Java-XML mapping is used as specified in the *Java Architecture for XML Binding* (JAXB) [Sun06b].

Due to the missing reflection support in C++, AWSM specifies a `getState()` method, which has to be implemented by the *AWSM service* developer in the gSOAP approach. In order to help developers identifying the necessary implementation state, an extended WSDL description is used, which contains a specification of the *AWSM service* facet's implementation-independent state (see Figure 3.13, lines 8–11). Such kind of WSDL description is automatically generated by the Axis-based prototype on the basis of specified Java annotations.

The last step of state transfer is setting the state of the target *AWSM service* (i.e., internalisation). The Axis-based prototype uses Java reflection in conjunction with annotations to automatically set the needed state. In the gSOAP prototype, the developer has to implement a facet-specific `setState()` method. There, the aforementioned WSDL state description can again be used to identify the needed implementation-independent state.

3.3.2.5 Dynamic Loading of Code

For supporting dynamic loading of code within the AWSM infrastructure, DCM is integrated into the `AWSMGenericFactory` (analogous to the AOM approach in Section 3.3.1.5). If the `AWSMGenericFactory` receives a `create()` request (see Figure 3.14, Step 1) and the code for the necessary *AWSM service* facet is locally unavailable, DCM (i.e., `DynamicLoader`) is queried for available implementations (Step 2). The *AWSM service* facet name and the application name are used to identify the code within DCM. If available, DCM loads the code and deploys a specific `AWSMFactory` (Step 3), which is able to deploy the needed *AWSM service* facet (Step 4 and 5). More details about DCM can be found in Section 4.1.

3.3.2.6 Identity and Addressing

As already mentioned in Section 3.2.1, the AXM design pattern ensures that a unique application identity is maintained even while fundamentally adapting the application (i.e., the *AWSM*

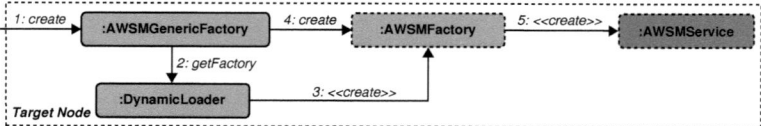

Figure 3.14: Dynamic loading of code with AWSM

service). Web services are in general uniquely identified by their service URI. The AWSM prototype embeds the unique *AWSM service* identifier (i.e., instanceID) into the *AWSM service* URI, which is encoded in a URI scheme as follows.

<serverURI>/<deploymentPath>/<applicationName>.<instanceID>[4]

With this scheme, multiple *AWSM service* instances of an application can be deployed on the same host.

AWSM uses the unique *AWSM service* identity to address the *AWSM service* independent of its facet and location. Therefore, a *location tracking service* manages current locations of available *AWSM services* (comparable to AOM; see Section 3.3.1.6). *AWSM services* initially register their current service address with the unique identity with a public service address at the location tracking service. The public address is used as a permanent Web service reference. All invocations are redirected by the Web service container using the location tracking service. Whenever a Web service changes its location, it has to notify the location tracking service about the new location (i.e., the reference is updated).

For improving the request performance of the Axis-based approach, an interceptor-based approach is used at the client-side. Therefore, the Java prototype provides an HTTPSender handler implementation for client-side interception of SOAP requests over HTTP. It has to be registered at the client, which results in every invocation passing through the interceptor's invoke() method. Within this method, the location tracking service is used for determining the current location of the *AWSM service* as described before. This mechanism allows forwarding requests if required. The current location of an *AWSM service* given in a redirect response is cached. Thus, subsequent invocations can directly be forwarded without redirection. A 404 Not Found response (e.g., triggered by another migration) leads to invoking the original service URI again.

---

[4]e.g., http://www.uulm.de:8080/axis/services/MMPClient.04daf796-5f69-4100-b0ea-29da3040d2d3 for an *AWSM service* implementing the mobile multimedia player client (see Section 2.2.2)

```
1  public abstract class AWSMServiceImpl extends BuiltInStatefulService implements AWSMService
   {
2    public void preAdaptation(){...}
3    public void postAdaptation(){...}
4    public String adapt(String xmlCriteria, String facFinderURI){...}
5    public String copy(String xmlCriteria, String facFinderURI){...}
6    public String move(String xmlCriteria, String facFinderURI){...}
7    public void remove(){...}
8  }
```

Figure 3.15: Abstract `AWSMServiceImpl` class (Java)

An alternative approach for addressing is based on P2P mechanisms. This can potentially solve typical issues of server-based solutions, such as scalability and manageability issues. The current location of a *AWSM service* is stored in a P2P network. The unique service identifier acts as the key to store and retrieve this information. Whenever the *AWSM service* changes its location, the current location is updated in the P2P network. If a service invocation fails due to the *AWSM service* being moved to another location, an AWSM-provided client-side interceptor is able to locate the current location via the P2P network and to transparently reinvoke the service at the actual location.

Within the gSOAP-based approach, the global `process_request()` method serving SOAP requests is again used to implement a server-side interceptor. This allows implementing a gSOAP-based location tracking service as well. Unfortunately, there is no support for implementing a client-side interceptor in gSOAP to improve forwarding performance with caching.

As already described in Section 3.2.2.4, all facets of an *AWSM service* should implement a common interface for client-transparency of fundamental *AWSM service* adaptation.

3.3.2.7 Development Support

For supporting the developer, AWSM provides an abstract `AWSMServiceImpl` class (see Figure 3.15). It contains generic code for introspection (`getState()` and `setState()` methods as part of the `BuiltInStatefulService` class on the basis of the introduced Java annotation), the generation of the globally unique identifier and the fundamental adaptation methods. Developers inherit this class to implement an *AWSM service*. Then, in addition to providing the pure application and fundamental adaptation logic, they only have to ensure the state consistency among different *AWSM service* facets.

The gSOAP prototype provides basic tool support. The methods `getState()` and `setState()` are generated on the basis of the WSDL state description (see Section 3.3.2.4). Additionally, the gSOAP implementation provides the fundamental adaptation code of an *AWSM service* as part of a shared object file, which can be used by developers.

3.4 Case Studies: AXM for Adaptive Applications in Mobile and UbiComp Scenarios

As part of this thesis, an AXM-based prototype implementation was developed for all scenarios presented in Section 2.2. The following sections show the respective implementations and provide measurements regarding their performance.

3.4.1 Cyber Foraging – Distributed Ray Tracing

As introduced in Section 2.2.1, the distributed ray tracing application leverages cyber foraging scenarios.

3.4.1.1 Implementation

Figure 3.16 shows a class diagram of the needed facets of the distributed ray tracing application. Three interfaces and their respective implementation classes represent the three required facets for preparation, rendering and presentation of the frame. The preparation facet (i.e., `Prepare` interface and `PrepareImpl` class) collects required data for the rendering process (i.e., title, description, light settings and sphere settings); the `renderJob()` method initiates the workflow. The rendering facet (i.e., `Job` interface and `JobImpl` class) renders the frame within the `render()` method. For this purpose, light and sphere settings are transferred with the fundamental adaptation into this facet. The rendered scene is stored in a `frame` variable. The last facet is the result facet (i.e., `Result` interface and `ResultImpl` class). There, the title, the description (entered into the first facet and passivated in the state store; see Section 3.2.2.3) and the frame are displayed in a GUI. All facets share a common `Status` interface, which can be used to monitor the application independent of the current facet and location.

Within the CORBA-based implementation on the basis of AOM, all three facet interfaces inherit the `LifeCycleObject` interface (specified within the IDL description). The implementation classes are described as IDL value types, which support the respective interface and inherit

3.4 Case Studies: AXM for Adaptive Applications in Mobile and UbiComp Scenarios

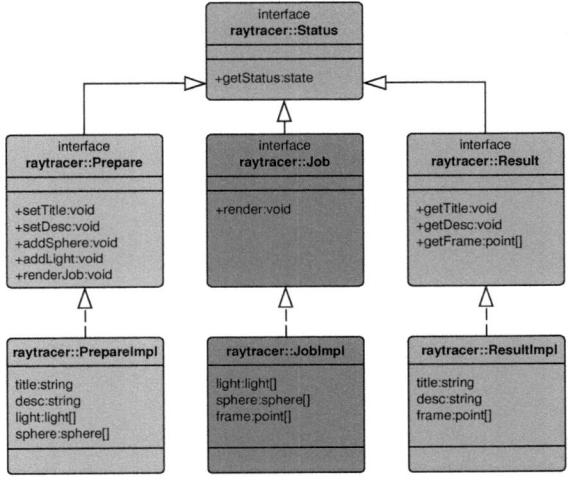

Figure 3.16: AXM implementation of a ray tracing application

`AOMObject` (which implicitly contains the code for internalisation, externalisation and life-cycle management). The implementation-independent state of each facet is specified as part of the IDL value type descriptions.

For the implementation with AWSM, all of the three corresponding *AWSM service* facet interfaces inherit the `AWSMService` interface containing the needed life-cycle methods. All implementations implement the respective interfaces and inherit the abstract class `AWSMServiceImpl`, which contains the life-cycle management code. The implementation-independent state is marked with Java annotations and as part of the WSDL descriptions as described in Section 3.3.2.4.

3.4.1.2 Performance Evaluation

This section presents an evaluation of the AOM and AWSM prototypes with respect to their particular performance and transferred network data volume. Figure 3.17 shows the evaluation

3 AXM: Architectural Design Pattern for Fundamentally Adaptive Applications

Name	CPU	RAM	Network	GCC	Java
Desktop	Intel Core2 Duo E8400 3.00GHz	4GB	100Mbit/s (LAN)	4.3.2	Sun 1.6.0_10-b33
EeePC	Intel Atom N270 1.60GHz	1GB	100Mbit/s (LAN)	4.2.4	Sun 1.6.0_06
N810	TI OMAP 2420 400 MHz	128MB	54 Mbit/s (WLAN)	3.4.4	CACAO 0.99.3

Figure 3.17: Evaluation hardware and software

Platform	Language	Invocation Time (ms)			
		AOM		AWSM	
		Factory Finder	State Store	Factory Finder	State Store
Desktop	Java	1.5 ± 0.2	1.6 ± 0.3	5.9 ± 1.2	6.9 ± 2.3
	C++	0.9 ± 0.2	1.0 ± 0.2	3.8 ± 2.4	4.8 ± 2.9
EeePC	Java	3.0 ± 0.7	3.1 ± 0.6	35.0 ± 5.7	229.0 ± 8.0
	C++	1.6 ± 0.3	1.6 ± 0.4	17.0 ± 4.1	26.1 ± 8.0
N810	Java	10.0 ± 1.9	10.1 ± 2.1	234.3 ± 26.1	653.7 ± 368.8
	C++	3.1 ± 0.5	3.2 ± 0.6	128.0 ± 19.1	137.6 ± 23.4

Figure 3.18: Invocation time at the factory finder and the state store

hardware in use: a powerful desktop machine, an Asus EeePC subnotebook and a resource-limited Nokia N810 Internet tablet. Such hardware represents typical hardware for the scenarios described in Section 2.2. Regarding AOM, the Java prototype runs with JacORB 2.1, while the C++ prototype uses Orbacus 4.3.0. For all AWSM evaluation cases the services run on top of Apache Axis 1.4 within Apache Tomcat 5.5.27 in the Java environment and gSOAP 2.7.10 in the C++ environment.

Invocation Times of Infrastructure Services To evaluate the infrastructures regarding invocation time, the time to search for factories at the factory finder and to store state at the state store were measured for both AXM systems. The respective methods (`find_factories()` and `store()`) were invoked with the same parameters 100 times and the average duration was measured with the standard deviation (see Figure 3.18). For the Java setup, the first measurement was removed due to JVM initialisation issues.

For the AWSM prototype, the differences between the C++ and Java implementations on the desktop machine are negligible (only 2ms in average). In contrast to this, on the EeePC and the N810, programming language differences have high impact on performance. On the N810, the standard deviation is relatively high for the state store invocation time. This results from the fact that the invocation times get higher with the invocation count due to the internal state store implementation as an XML repository. There, invoking `store()` appends an XML node

3.4 Case Studies: AXM for Adaptive Applications in Mobile and UbiComp Scenarios

Adaptive Object Migration		Duration (s) — Source -> Target			
		Java -> Java	Java -> C++	C++ -> Java	C++ -> C++
Setup: Desktop -> Desktop					
1 Local Adaptation	(Pre. -> Job)	0.107 ± 0.004	0.105 ± 0.004	0.003 ± 0.000	0.002 ± 0.000
2 Migration	(Pre.)	0.113 ± 0.007	0.109 ± 0.006	0.003 ± 0.000	0.002 ± 0.000
3 Adaptation	(Pre. -> Job)	0.111 ± 0.006	0.108 ± 0.005	0.003 ± 0.000	0.002 ± 0.000
Setup: Desktop -> EeePC					
4 Migration	(Job)	0.126 ± 0.005	0.114 ± 0.007	0.003 ± 0.000	0.003 ± 0.000
5 Adaptation	(Job -> Res.)	0.128 ± 0.004	0.118 ± 0.008	0.003 ± 0.000	0.003 ± 0.000
Setup: Desktop -> N810					
6 Migration	(Job)	0.170 ± 0.009	0.139 ± 0.007	0.141 ± 0.008	0.059 ± 0.002
7 Adaptation	(Job -> Res.)	0.173 ± 0.011	0.141 ± 0.009	0.144 ± 0.007	0.059 ± 0.003
Setup: EeePC -> Desktop					
8 Local Adaptation	(Pre. -> Job)	0.139 ± 0.006	0.131 ± 0.007	0.008 ± 0.000	0.008 ± 0.000
9 Migration	(Pre.)	0.135 ± 0.007	0.124 ± 0.006	0.007 ± 0.000	0.007 ± 0.000
10 Adaptation	(Pre. -> Job)	0.134 ± 0.004	0.123 ± 0.005	0.007 ± 0.000	0.007 ± 0.000
Setup: N810 -> Desktop					
11 Local Adaptation	(Pre. -> Job)	2.700 ± 0.247	1.120 ± 0.065	0.147 ± 0.007	0.066 ± 0.003
12 Migration	(Pre.)	0.971 ± 0.053	0.920 ± 0.044	0.065 ± 0.002	0.065 ± 0.003
13 Adaptation	(Pre. -> Job)	0.970 ± 0.052	0.919 ± 0.048	0.064 ± 0.002	0.064 ± 0.002

Figure 3.19: AOM: Duration of fundamental adaptation of the ray tracing application facets

to the XML repository and Java XML processing is slow on the N810. The AOM prototypes are considerably faster compared to the AWSM entities. This results from the fact that the AWSM prototypes use XML while the AOM entities use standard CORBA binary CDR streams for communication. For AOM, the differences between C++ and Java entities are comparatively small. Even on the N810, both AOM entities provide reasonable performance.

To sum up, the AWSM infrastructure should run on powerful machines (the more powerful they are, the less impact they have on fundamental adaptation time). For the following evaluations the desktop machines host the required infrastructure services. Thus, there is no need to differentiate between Java and C++ infrastructure services anymore but particular attention is given to the differences between source and target platform for fundamental adaptation. In the same way, the desktop machines host the infrastructure entities for the following AOM evaluations to gain comparable results with respect to the AWSM prototypes.

Fundamental Adaptation Duration with AOM Regarding fundamental adaptation performance, the time needed to fundamentally adapt the ray tracing application facets was measured. Figure 3.19 shows the results for the AOM prototypes. The evaluation cases represent the scenario of the ray tracing application as described in Section 2.2.1. To gain more realistic results, the time needed to fundamentally adapt a specific facet was measured 100 times. For the Java measurements, the first measurement was removed due to JVM initialisation issues. Figure 3.19 shows the average time needed and the standard deviation for each evaluation case.

Overall, the results show that a pure Java setting provides the worst performance while a pure C++ variant has the best performance. Moreover, a Java to C++ setting is slightly faster than a pure Java variant and a C++ to Java setting is slightly slower than a pure C++ variant. The source platform performance has the most influence on the overall fundamental adaptation performance. This results from the fact that the most demanding operations for fundamental adaptation are processed at the source node (see Section 3.3.1.2).

It is expectable that the desktop to desktop setting (Figure 3.19, 1–3) provides the best performance in general, while settings with the EeePC (4–5 and 8–10) and the N810 (6–7 and 11–13) are considerably slower. Yet, at first glance, it is not obvious that the pure migration of the **Prepare** facet (2, 9 and 12) is slightly slower than fundamental adaptation with migration to the Job facet (3, 10 and 13). This results from the fact that the **Prepare** facet requires loading more state than the Job facet (see Figure 3.16). More state requires more state transfer and processing, which results in the slightly higher migration time. In contrast to this, the pure migration of the Job facet is faster than the fundamental adaptation with migration to the Result facet (4–7) because the Result facet comprises more state that has to be loaded. Finally, local fundamental adaptation on the N810 (11) with the Java prototype as source platform is considerably slower than the fundamental adaptation with migration from the desktop to the N810 (7) due to the firm resource restrictions on the N810 device (128MB RAM being almost fully used at runtime).

Fundamental Adaptation Duration with AWSM For the AWSM prototypes, the measurements regarding the time needed to fundamentally adapt the ray tracing application facets were repeated under the same conditions as in the AOM evaluation before. Figure 3.20 shows the results.

In each evaluation case the pure Java setting provides the worst performance while the pure C++ variant shows the best performance. Moreover, a C++ to Java setting is slightly faster than a pure Java variant and a Java to C++ setting is slightly slower than a pure C++ variant. In contrast to the AOM evaluation, the *target* platform performance has most influence on the overall fundamental adaptation performance. This is due to the fact that deployment takes most of the time in the AWSM prototypes. Especially in the Java case, Apache Axis provides very

3.4 Case Studies: AXM for Adaptive Applications in Mobile and UbiComp Scenarios

Adaptive Web Service Migration		Duration (s) — Source -> Target			
		Java -> Java	Java -> C++	C++ -> Java	C++ -> C++
Setup: Desktop -> Desktop					
1 Local Adaptation	(Pre. -> Job)	1.979 ± 0.107	0.972 ± 0.018	1.950 ± 0.278	0.943 ± 0.003
2 Migration	(Pre.)	2.007 ± 0.086	0.997 ± 0.022	2.003 ± 0.079	0.958 ± 0.005
3 Adaptation	(Pre. -> Job)	2.000 ± 0.084	0.992 ± 0.017	1.969 ± 0.271	0.950 ± 0.004
Setup: Desktop -> EeePC					
4 Migration	(Job)	9.623 ± 0.629	5.322 ± 0.575	9.338 ± 0.870	5.128 ± 0.363
5 Adaptation	(Job -> Res.)	9.718 ± 0.896	5.338 ± 0.609	9.497 ± 0.771	5.236 ± 0.446
Setup: Desktop -> N810					
6 Migration	(Job)	51.938 ± 0.572	28.267 ± 0.349	51.614 ± 0.570	28.057 ± 0.258
7 Adaptation	(Job -> Res.)	52.115 ± 0.709	29.288 ± 0.376	51.776 ± 0.540	28.231 ± 0.376
Setup: EeePC -> Desktop					
8 Local Adaptation	(Pre. -> Job)	9.913 ± 0.814	5.378 ± 0.658	9.780 ± 0.520	5.237 ± 0.735
9 Migration	(Pre.)	2.081 ± 0.097	1.153 ± 0.170	2.056 ± 0.097	0.978 ± 0.007
10 Adaptation	(Pre. -> Job)	2.068 ± 0.084	1.146 ± 0.115	2.011 ± 0.99	0.954 ± 0.003
Setup: N810 -> Desktop					
11 Local Adaptation	(Pre. -> Job)	64.122 ± 0.679	29.442 ± 1.108	56.837 ± 0.966	28.478 ± 0.611
12 Migration	(Pre.)	3.391 ± 0.474	1.806 ± 0.399	2.115 ± 0.092	1.055 ± 0.020
13 Adaptation	(Pre. -> Job)	3.254 ± 0.402	1.793 ± 0.380	2.102 ± 0.099	1.053 ± 0.022

Figure 3.20: AWSM: Duration of fundamental adaptation of the ray tracing application facets

poor performance regarding deployment [SKHR08]. On the desktop machine, Axis deployment of the particular *AWSM services* implementing the measured performance cases takes in average 0.586 ± 0.042 seconds. Thus, deployment consumes 17–30% of overall time. On the EeePC the average deployment duration is 2.612 ± 0.585 seconds (i.e., 26–27% of overall time) and on the N810 it is 50.665 ± 3.723 seconds (i.e., 79–97% of overall time). The C++ prototype implementation compiles the target Web service from the source code on the fly if the compiled code is unavailable. This is part of the deployment at the target location and enables support for arbitrary platforms if the source code is available and compilable at the target.

Again, it is obvious that the desktop to desktop setting (Figure 3.20, 1–3) provides the best performance and settings with the EeePC (4–5 and 8–10) and the N810 (6–7 and 11–13) are considerably slower. Yet, for the same reasons as in the AOM evaluation, the pure migration of the Prepare facet (2, 9 and 12) is slightly slower than fundamental adaptation with migration to the Job facet (3, 10 and 13), while the pure migration of the Job facet is faster than the fundamental adaptation with migration to the Result facet for both settings (4–7). Finally, due to the firm resource restrictions on the N810 device (128MB RAM being almost fully used at runtime), the local fundamental adaptation with Java as target platform is considerably slow.

Ray Tracing Application	Network Data Transfer (kB)		Code Size (kB)	
	AOM	AWSM	AOM (Java/C++)	AWSM (Java/C++)
Migration (Pre.)	6.110	9.736	15.625 / 52.735	1.532 / 9.376
Adaptation (Pre. -> Job)	6.055	9.485	13.737 / 48.893[5]	0.753 / 8.340[5]
Migration (Job)	11.077	16.585	13.737 / 48.893[5]	0.753 / 8.340[5]
Adaptation (Job -> Res.)	11.081	16.641	14.571 / 49.637	0.779 / 8.653

Figure 3.21: Network data volume of fundamental adaptation of the ray tracing application

Fundamental Adaptation Duration Summary To sum up, for the AOM prototypes the performance of the *source* platform has the most impact on fundamental adaptation duration, while the performance of the *target* platform has the most impact for the AWSM prototypes. For both AXM systems, the C++ prototype is faster than the Java prototype. The results with desktop and EeePC as target platforms show reasonable performance while the Java setting on the N810 provides weak performance.

Yet, it is difficult to estimate if migration makes sense for a particular case as this is highly application dependent. For the ray tracing application, ray tracing on the N810 in general takes even longer than migrating the service on the desktop machine and ray tracing there. However, this depends on the actual data set for ray tracing. To improve the evaluation results for the AWSM Java prototype, deployment time has to be decreased. This could be done by porting AWSM to a more efficient Web service container for mobile devices, such as SoapME, which is introduced in Section 4.4. The C++ prototype automatically provides improved performance if the compiled code is already available at the target location (this compiled code could also be loaded with DCM as described in Section 4.1).

Transferred Network Data Volume The author also measured the transferred network data volume for the prior test cases for both AXM systems. Figure 3.21 shows the results with the respective facet code size (without the required basic AOM or AWSM functionality, which is assumed to be available at all target factories). This is essential if the application code is unavailable at the target and thus has to be loaded at runtime with DCM.

The **Prepare** facet has the maximum code size because it contains the functionality to initialise the ray tracing configuration data. In comparison to the pure migration of the **Prepare** facet, the fundamental adaptation to the **Job** facet requires transferring a slightly lower network data volume because the **Job** facet needs less state variables to load (**title** and **description** are

---

[5]without ray tracing logic (code size highly depends on the required ray tracing functionality)

3.4 Case Studies: AXM for Adaptive Applications in Mobile and UbiComp Scenarios

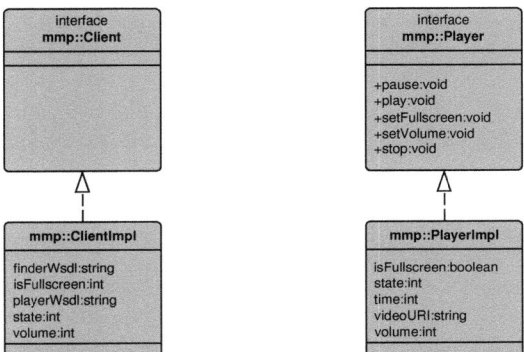

Figure 3.22: AWSM implementation of mobile multimedia player application components

passivated). The `Job` facet has the lowest code size due to the fact that it provides only one method to run the ray tracing job (this method is actually a dummy method in the prototype; the overall code size highly depends on the ray tracing logic in use). The migration of the `Job` facet requires more state transfer because the rendered scene is transferred (for the evaluation only a very small dummy frame with a size of about 5kB is transferred). The fundamental adaptation from the `Job` facet into the `Result` facet again requires slightly more network data transfer due to the fact that parts of the initial configuration data are activated again. In comparison to the `Job` facet, the `Result` facet has slightly more code size as it provides more methods. In comparison to AWSM, the transfer volume of the AOM prototype is lower. This results from the fact that AWSM uses XML-based SOAP communication, while AOM communicates with standard CORBA CDR streams that use a binary transfer format. The code size of the AOM implementations is bigger in comparison to the AWSM ones due to the fact that *AOM object* implementations contain several (CORBA-) generated skeleton classes. Overall, the required network data volume is reasonable, especially if the code is already available at the target location (then, there is no need to transfer any code at all).

3.4.2 Follow-me – Mobile Multimedia Player

Figure 3.22 shows the AWSM implementation of the needed components for the mobile multimedia player scenario (see Section 2.2.2). In contrast to the implementation of the previous section, both components do *not* represent application facets due to the fact that the application does not provide fundamental adaptivity regarding functionality (i.e., interface).

As the client application is the remote control (i.e., `Client` interface and `ClientImpl` class), it is not remotely accessible. Still, it is implemented as an *AWSM service* to provide mobility. The implementation-independent state consists of the factory finder URI in use, the player URI to control, the client state (e.g., *video playing*) and play information (i.e., full screen and volume). This state is stored and restored whenever the client application migrates.

For being remotely controllable, the player (i.e., `Player` interface and `PlayerImpl` class) provides its functionality as a Web service. There, basic functionality for playing, pausing and stopping the video is offered. Additionally, the volume can be changed and the video can be set to full screen. The implementation-independent state comprises the video state (e.g., *playing*), the current playing time, the video URI, the volume and if full screen is enabled. This state is needed whenever the player reinitialises the video with the prior setting after migration.

The mobile multimedia player application components provide fundamental adaptation in terms of the respective implementation. For instance, the client component is able to run as a Standard Widget Toolkit (SWT)-based GUI application on a standard device. Yet, on a mobile device running only Java ME, an alternative implementation on the basis of the Mobile Information Device Profile (MIDP) is used. For the player component, there are alternative implementations based on the Java QuickTime API for Java [Ada05], the JMF [Sun02] and the MMAPI [Sun06e]. An appropriate implementation is dynamically selected according to the installed media framework on the migration target.

There are further components needed for the mobile multimedia application to work properly, such as a context service (see Section 4.2). Due to the fact that with these components it is impossible to compare the performance with respect to the measurements of the previous sections, the author only measured the migration time of the player component implemented in Java between two standard notebooks (Intel Core2 Duo 2 GHz, 1 GB RAM), which are connected via 54Mbit WLAN. In this setting, migration takes only between one and two seconds. This is a reasonable delay. In particular, the migrating player plays the video until the `create()` method returns from the factory. Thus, for the user the *felt delay* is even smaller. However, the part of the media stream, which is presented at the original location during the migration process, is replayed at the target location again. This is due to the fact that the player state has to be transferred during migration but it allows the user refocusing the presentation.

3.4 Case Studies: AXM for Adaptive Applications in Mobile and UbiComp Scenarios

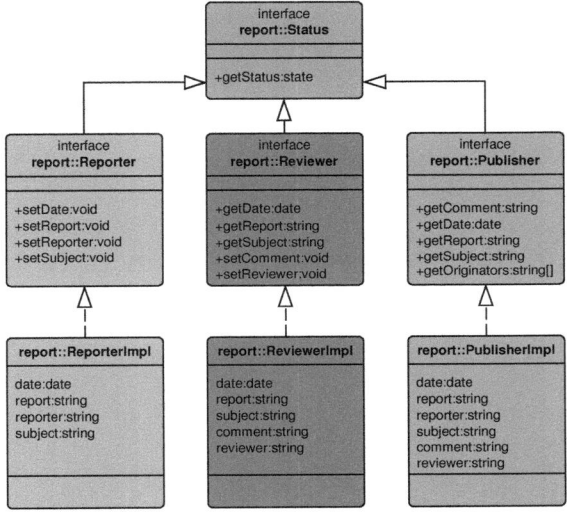

Figure 3.23: AXM implementation of report application

3.4.3 Crisis Management – Report Application

As already introduced in Section 2.2.3, the report application provides means for documenting a crisis situation.

3.4.3.1 Implementation

Figure 3.23 shows the implementation concept for the report application. The three interfaces and their implementing classes represent the three roles of the mobile report workflow: the reporter creates, the reviewer checks and the publisher handles reports (e.g., rescue coordination centre as described in Section 2.2.3). The reporter facet (i.e., Reporter interface and ReporterImpl class) allows entering data in a GUI to create a report with corresponding data (i.e., creation date, reporter, subject). The reviewer facet (i.e., Reviewer interface and ReviewerImpl class) provides means to check the report according to its importance. Therefore, the report itself, the subject and the creation date are transferred to implement migration (the name of the reporter is not transferred to allow anonymous reviewing). The reviewer is able to add a comment and the reviewer name is stored for documentation. The last facet implements the publisher role (i.e., `Publisher` interface and `PublisherImpl` class). The publisher is able to access all data entered by the reporter and the reviewer (here, the full state is retrieved from the state store). Like in the ray tracer application, all facets share a common `Status` interface, which can be used to monitor the application (See Section 3.2.2.4).

All facet interfaces of the CORBA-based implementation for AOM inherit the `LifeCycleObject` interface. Within the IDL description, the implementation classes are described as value types supporting the respective interface and inheriting `AOMObject` (implicitly contains code for internalisation, externalisation and life-cycle management). Like in the ray tracer example, the implementation-independent state of each facet is specified within the IDL value type descriptions.

All of the corresponding *AWSM service* facet interfaces of the implementation for AWSM inherit the `AWSMService` interface, which contains the life-cycle methods. All implementations implement the respective interfaces and inherit the abstract class `AWSMServiceImpl` implementing the life-cycle management. Again, the implementation-independent state is marked with Java annotations as described in Section 3.3.2.4.

3.4.3.2 Performance Evaluation

Due to the fact that the evaluation results regarding fundamental adaptation duration in comparison to the ray tracing application are very similar, this thesis omits this evaluation for the report application.

Transferred Network Data Volume Nevertheless, the author evaluated the required network data transfer volume for both AXM systems. Figure 3.24 shows the results. The pure `Reporter` migration requires transferring more data via the network than the fundamental adaptation to the `Reviewer` facet because the `Reporter` facet comprising less state variables in comparison to the `Reviewer` facet. Thus, pure migration duration is slightly higher than fundamental adaptation. For the pure `Reviewer` migration more data is transferred compared to the fundamental adaptation of the `Reporter`. This is due to the `Reviewer` facet comprising more state variables being passivated. In comparison to the fundamental adaptation to the `Publisher` facet, pure migration of the `Reviewer` facet requires less data transfer due to more state being activated in the `Publisher` facet. Again, this leads to fundamental adaptation duration being slightly higher

Report Application	Network Data Transfer (kB)		Code Size (kB)	
	AOM	AWSM	AOM (Java/C++)	AWSM (Java/C++)
Migration (Rep.)	6.212	10.196	14.199 / 44.938	1.790 / 8.662
Adaptation (Rep. –> Rev.)	6.123	10.112	12.729 / 41.748	1.687 / 7.307
Migration (Rev.)	6.248	10.280	12.729 / 41.748	1.687 / 7.307
Adaptation (Rev. –> Pub.)	6.327	10.369	13.406 / 43.181	1.716 / 7.344

Figure 3.24: Network data volume of fundamental adaptation of the report application

than pure migration. AOM leads to less network data transfer compared to AWSM. This results from using binary encoded CDR in CORBA while using XML for Web services. The code size of all facets for the respective prototypes is comparable; the reporter facet requires most code because it provides functionality to enter data. Again, the code size of the AOM implementations is bigger in comparison to the AWSM ones due to the fact that *AOM object* implementations contain several generated skeleton classes. Overall, the transferred network data volume is reasonable, especially if the code is already available at the target location.

3.5 Summary

To sum up, AXM introduces a novel architectural design pattern. In contrast to related work, it supports developing adaptive applications by providing highly flexible means to fundamentally adapt applications in terms of the available state, provided functionality, implementation in use and the current location (i.e., migration). The AXM pattern is independent of the concrete implementation infrastructure and platform. It only requires support for implementation-language–independent interfaces and data structure descriptions that can be mapped to different implementation languages. This has been proved by two prototypes, the CORBA-based AOM system and the Web-service–based AWSM platform, which are both implemented without any changes regarding the respective middleware platform. For both, there are interoperable implementations for Java and C++. For showing the benefit of the approach, details are provided on implementing the introduced example applications for mobile and UbiComp scenarios on the basis of the AXM design pattern. The evaluation of these applications shows that the implementation platform (i.e., CORBA vs. Web services) has a high impact on the performance. Nevertheless, all prototypes show reasonable performance for most[6] settings.

---

[6]The evaluation settings with the Nokia N810 device running Java as target platform provide weak performance. Yet, the evaluation shows that using C++ as an alternative target platform on the N810 considerably improves performance.

As already mentioned before, this thesis advocates the use of Web services as communication technology in mobile and UbiComp scenarios as these have already achieved acceptance in standard environments. Additionally, there is already promising work on Web services providing reasonable communication between heterogeneous sensors [LKNZ08]. Thus, for the following chapters, AWSM represents the default implementation of AXM.

The development of adaptive applications on the basis of the prototypes is a reasonable task for experienced software developers using the respective basic development support. Nevertheless, AXM-based application development is still quite complex due to its highly flexible fundamental adaptation support. Thus, further support to ease application development with the AXM design pattern and to ensure application consistency (e.g., state consistency between different application facets) is desirable. Chapter 5 introduces a model-driven approach for easing the development of *AWSM services*. This approach could also be adopted to support the development of *AOM objects*.

For implementing sophisticated applications for mobile and UbiComp scenarios there is a need for further infrastructure support, such as dynamic loading of code and support for application context. The following chapter presents such infrastructure support. In conjunction with the AXM prototypes, these services contribute to a powerful mobile and UbiComp platform.

4

Infrastructure Services for Mobile and Ubiquitous Computing Environments

This chapter introduces novel infrastructure services that support sophisticated applications in mobile and UbiComp scenarios. These are a service for the dynamic management of code, a generic context service, an entity discovery service (i.e., locating users, devices and services) and a lightweight Web service container. The following sections present these services in detail with an elaborate discussion of the respective related work.

4.1 Dynamic Management of Code

Dynamic management of code is a crucial and often neglected part of distributed systems facing increasing dynamics, complexity and heterogeneity. Mobile and UbiComp scenarios even strengthen this trend of distributed systems. As the local availability of suitable code cannot be assumed in such environments, this thesis proposes a generic concept for a decentralised *dynamic code management* (DCM) infrastructure in Section 4.1.3. The whole process of publication, lookup, implementation selection and the final loading of platform-specific code is decentralised and requires only basic P2P functionality. In addition to code selection on the basis of functional needs, the concept supports the selection process with specifying non-functional requirements as well. This is an essential issue in mobile and UbiComp scenarios (Section 4.1.2 presents an in-depth discussion of the necessity of non-functional properties). In contrast to related work, such as the centralised approach proposed by *Kapitza and Hauck* [KH03], the novel DCM infrastructure allows any participating peer in the network to offer and obtain platform-specific code. This thesis presents a JXTA-based prototype for dynamic management of platform-specific code that is built on the basis of the generic concept.

OSGi [OSG07a] emerged as a de-facto standard[1] for modularising and managing all kinds of complex Java-based software, such as car infotainment systems, integrated development environments (IDEs, e.g., Eclipse) and application servers (e.g., WebSphere). *Concierge* [RA07] is a very lightweight implementation of the OSGi specification that especially supports mobile and UbiComp scenarios. Hence, Section 4.1.4 shows an integration of the code management service with OSGi. This integration allows centralised and decentralised dynamic discovery, selection and deployment of OSGi components and services with their respective dependencies. It supports automatic component selection by functional and non-functional properties. The service is transparently integrated into the OSGi system and does not require any changes to the OSGi platform. The end of the section proposes an integration of AWSM with the OSGi-based DCM service.

The following section gives a broad overview on related work regarding the dynamic management of code.

4.1.1 Related Work

Many code deployment systems are server-based and rely on a central repository. Thus, the following systems suffer from well-known limitations of server-based solutions, such as high administrative effort and lack of scalability. A P2P approach can solve these issues and still include server nodes. *None* of the presented approaches supports the automatic selection of the best-fitting software according to non-functional requirements. Yet, Section 4.1.2 highlights the necessity of non-functional properties in context of this thesis.

Kapitza and Hauck [KH03] present the Dynamic Loading Service (DLS), a CORBA service for dynamic code loading. It allows the installation of locally unavailable code on the basis of an IDL

---

[1]OSGi enjoys wide industry acceptance as it facilitates lightweight techniques for dynamic component updates and automatic code dependency resolution during system runtime.

interface name. Therefore, a local DLS client queries a central repository and returns available implementations. Unlike the approach of this thesis, implementation selection is only supported by simple policies and dependent code is not resolved automatically.

Java Web Start [Sun05b] is a deployment system for Java software on the basis of the Java Network Launching Protocol. Requirements of the application and the needed code are described with XML. A Java Web Start client is able to install the application by evaluating the XML description. Yet, Java Web Start is restricted to Java and targets the deployment of complete applications. Thus, it is not suited for dynamic and incremental dependency resolution as needed in the context of mobile and UbiComp scenarios.

Paal et al. propose a distributed code loading infrastructure based on multiple application repositories that can be dynamically queried by a custom application loader [PKF05]. The system offers fine-grained code loading based on *class collections*, which are represented by class subsets of a Java archive. However, the system is limited to the Java programming language and application repositories have to be preconfigured at initial deployment time to enable code loading.

A P2P-based architecture for remote loading of Java classes is described by *Parker and Cleary* [PC03]. This approach shows an alternative way to the standard Java class loader mechanism and is exemplarily realised using JXTA. In comparison to the approach of this thesis, it lacks the flexibility to describe and to search for suitable program code and is restricted to Java.

There is also related work with respect to dynamic management of code for modularised applications on the basis of components [Szy02]. For instance, the *SATIN* component model was developed to support reconfiguration of mobile applications at runtime [ZME06]. It provides discovery mechanisms to search for available components. New components can be integrated into the application by installing or migrating them to the local host. Yet, the approach is restricted to a proprietary component framework.

In context of OSGi, a central code server is provided by the OSGi Bundle Repository (OBR) [OSG06]. OBR is based on a Web server providing an XML file describing available bundles. This XML can be parsed by clients at runtime. Yet, current clients do not support dynamic changes. Unlike the approach of this thesis, OBR does not support queries without the fully-qualified bundle name and thus does not support discovery on the basis of keywords or other criteria. A simple distributed OBR was presented by *Frenot et al.* [FR05]. However, only selection and loading of bundles based on pure Java package dependencies but no selection

4 Infrastructure Services for Mobile and Ubiquitous Computing Environments

based on service (i.e., application) dependencies is supported. Just as with the OBR, bundles have to be installed explicitly.

4.1.2 Necessity of Non-functional Property Support

Before deployment it is necessary to evaluate if a certain implementation code suits the needs of an application, which should be deployed. This applies to all candidates with the required functional support. For an improved resource usage a dynamic code management platform should neither require the loading nor the deployment of implementation code for verifying if a certain implementation suits application needs. Instead, it should support this process by representing all kinds of non-functional properties in the same way as functional and compatibility properties. Therefore, it is necessary to represent non-functional properties as values that can be compared and rated. Thus, there has to be an evaluation function (e.g., a benchmark) that provides a value for rating and comparing implementations of the same functionality. The evaluation function and the conditions for performing the evaluation have to be agreed among all implementation providers. This is a non-trivial requirement but it enables to reason about non-functional properties. Additionally, there has to be a document outlining the procedure to measure the required non-functional properties. If for some reasons (e.g., an open system) different measurement settings are used, an ontology, for instance on the basis of OWL [W3C04a], could be used to gain a common understanding of the general evaluation conditions.

4.1.2.1 Analysis

As part of this thesis, the non-functional properties *performance* and *resource demand* were analysed on the basis of three different implementations of the OSGi Hypertext Transfer Protocol (HTTP) service [OSG07a].

Providing information via HTTP is needed for various kinds of applications. Consequently, an HTTP implementation is needed for different general conditions, such as to provide a basic location service on an embedded device. On a server system, the service can be used to serve all kinds of interactive applications that are concurrently accessed by a large number of users. In both use cases, an HTTP service has to be provided but there are different non-functional requirements for the respective implementations. In the first case on the embedded device, the service implementation should be lean and less resource consuming. In the second case on the powerful device, it should provide good performance and scale up to a large number of users.

Analysed Bundle	Requests/s	Memory Demand (kB)	Code Size (kB)
NanoHTTPD	289	19.6	22
Knopflerfish HTTP	334	33.2	126
Knopflerfish HTTP with Native Proxy	399	1613.2[2]	155[3]

Figure 4.1: Performance and memory consumption of OSGi HTTP implementations

For the following analysis three different HTTP service implementations were considered, each having different advantages under certain conditions and demands:

- A simple HTTP service based on NanoHTTPD [Elo08]. NanoHTTPD comprises only a single Java class. It has a very low footprint in terms of memory and code size. The drawback of NanoHTTPD is the comparable low performance due to the lack of multi-threading support.

- Knopflerfish HTTP as an average OSGi HTTP service implementation

- Knopflerfish HTTP extended by an additional server-side caching proxy. The idea is to offload the transfer of static files from the Java Virtual Machine (JVM). This improves performance but the drawback of this implementation is its dependency on native code for the caching proxy (i.e., to the Linux operating system).

4.1.2.2 Analysing Performance

Like most non-functional properties, performance is complex to measure. Measurements highly depend on the configuration and on the benchmarks with their settings. A dynamic code management platform should not make any assumptions about how or what kind of values are measured to characterise the performance of a component. It should just require information to determine these values. Thus, an implementation provider should be able to gain the necessary information to describe a component in a complete way. For instance, there are approaches to model the evaluation conditions for software performance using OWL, such as proposed by *Lera et al.* [LJP06].

In the context of this analysis the *httperf* tool [MJ98] was used to measure the performance of the HTTP service implementations in terms of requests per second. Two machines with a 3.2GHz

---
[2] 33.2kB (JVM) + 1580kB (ext.)
[3] 126kB (Bundle) + 29kB (ext.)

4 Infrastructure Services for Mobile and Ubiquitous Computing Environments

CPU and 1024Mb RAM running Sun JDK 1.5_09 served as evaluation platform (i.e., client and server machine). Figure 4.1 shows the results. As expected, NanoHTTPD provides the slowest implementation due to its missing support for multi-threading. The standard Knopflerfish HTTP service is slightly faster. Yet, it is not as fast as the proxy-extended variant.

4.1.2.3 Analysing Resource Demand

Resource demand has various dimensions, such as memory, disk space, CPU and bandwidth. Additionally, logical resources, such as open files and sockets and even software licences can be accounted. Yet, this section focuses on memory demand as it is an important criterion to determine if a certain implementation is executable on a given resource-restricted device, such as a mobile phone or a PDA. Therefore, the memory usage of the deployed implementation was measured. Figure 4.1 outlines the results. NanoHTTPD needs only 19.6kB as only 43 classes of the implementation and the Java standard library have to be loaded and instantiated. Due to providing more features, such as support for multi-threading and object pool support, the Knopflerfish service demands 33.2kB memory. Finally, the proxy-extended variant uses the same amount of memory inside the JVM as the Knopflerfish implementation but it needs 1580kB of additional memory for the proxy as a native process.

4.1.2.4 Scenario

Considering the aforementioned three implementations, a dynamic code management platform should be able to select a suitable implementation depending on performance requirements and resource demand (i.e., memory demand). There should be default priorities that are defined by the developer. For instance, on powerful machines, performance should be rated higher than resource consumption. This leads to an implementation primarily being selected on the basis of requests per second; then, resource consumption is taken into account.

On an average machine (e.g., desktop or notebook), the proxy-extended variant is selected as it provides the best performance. This implementation has specific system requirements as it includes native code that is only executable on a Linux system. If the requesting system runs a different operating system the standard Knopflerfish HTTP implementation is loaded. On resource-limited devices, such as mobile phones and PDAs, resource demand is rated higher than performance. This leads to the NanoHTTPD implementation being loaded.

4.1.2.5 Discussion

To sum up, support for non-functional properties is essential for a sophisticated dynamic code management platform. Especially in the case that multiple functionally-equivalent implementations are available, taking non-functional requirements into account can improve system performance and allows resource-aware implementation selection.

Yet, there has to be a standardised procedure (e.g., a benchmark) for making certain kinds of non-functional properties (e.g., performance and resource demand) measurable and therefore accountable during implementation selection. The outlined scenario assumes that all implementations are evaluated in context of the same environment setting. This is applicable for small scenarios but might be complicated in open distributed systems, in which all kinds of companies and open source projects are able to provide implementations. Today, for instance, a Web server is selected based on features and performance. In most cases, performance is either advertised by the project itself or—if available—by using standard benchmarks. This way, the approach of this thesis integrates what could be called current-best-practice in an automated code deployment process.

Additionally, it should be noted that all kinds of benchmarks assume certain scenarios, which might not apply for the current deployment situation (e.g., if the memory footprint is measured under low load but the deployed component is actually under high load most of the time). Yet, the author advocates that considering non-functional properties during deployment definitely improves the selection process in contrast to a selection without this information. For certain corner cases the evaluation function has to be adapted and extended but the approach of this thesis automatically improves the general case.

4.1.3 Generic Infrastructure for Decentralised Dynamic Management of Platform-specific Code

The following sections introduce a generic and decentralised peer-to-peer-based lookup, selection and loading process for dynamic management of code with taking functional as well as non-functional properties into account. It allows multiple parties to independently and non-reliably provide implementations for certain functionality. Section 4.1.3.3 shows a JXTA [Gon01] implementation on the basis of this generic concept. JXTA is used because of its flexibility: it allows replacing routing mechanisms (e.g., unstructured topology replaced by structured topology or centralised approach) without having to change the application itself (i.e., the prototype).

4 Infrastructure Services for Mobile and Ubiquitous Computing Environments

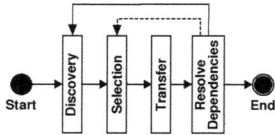

Figure 4.2: Process of automatically loading implementation code

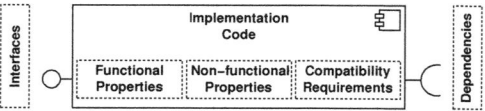

Figure 4.3: Description of implementation code

4.1.3.1 Generic Decentralised Dynamic Management of Code

This section elaborates on the properties and requirements that have to be considered for *dynamic code management* (DCM). Then, it introduces the basic infrastructure and outlines the basic workflow to publish, lookup and select particular implementations.

Dynamic Management of Code and Properties for Implementation Selection For providing automatic and dynamic loading of implementation code at runtime, a code management platform has to provide several functions (see Figure 4.2). First, implementation code has to be automatically *discovered* according to a given description (see below). Appropriate implementations have to be automatically *selected* and *transferred* to the local environment. Last, code *dependencies* have to be automatically resolved. If they cannot be resolved, a backtracking mechanism should load an alternative implementation of the previous selection if possible.

To automate the entire loading process it should run without user interaction. Thus, for dynamic loading of appropriate code at runtime, implementations have to be described with metadata. The author identified categories of properties and requirements that have to be satisfied or at least taken into account during the selection process (see Figure 4.3).

The *interface* determines the implemented functionality of an application at programming language level. Yet, for allowing the generic specification of functionality in a programming-language–independent manner, the interface has to be specified on the basis of a generic interface description language, such as CORBA IDL or WSDL.

Functional properties express additional functional aspects beyond the bare provision of an interface, such as the supported middleware platform. Implementations of the same functionality might also possess certain *non-functional properties* that specify quality-of-service aspects, such as timing behaviour and resource consumption. It is hard to identify a generic set of functional and non-functional properties that apply to a major number of applications. Thus, a dynamic code management platform should provide a flexible interface that enables applications to introduce code for custom evaluation.

Due to the fact that functionality can be implemented in various programming languages (e.g., Java and C++) and for specific run-time environments (e.g., Linux and Windows), particular *compatibility requirements* for a certain implementation have to be considered as well, such as the required programming language and execution environment. *Kapitza and Hauck* [KH03] outlined that such compatibility requirements define a limited set of properties (e.g., compiler, processor and operating system). Thus, it can be automatically determined whether an implementation is executable in the context of a requesting application.

Last, implementation code can have *dependencies* on other code, such as required libraries.

Basic Infrastructure For dynamic decentralised management of code, the author proposes an infrastructure that is composed of three basic entities.

A *dynamic loader* provides an interface for requesting locally unavailable functionality. This entity is able to discover, select and integrate an appropriate implementation into the address space of a requesting application.

The discovery process is supported by an *implementation repository* that stores information about available implementation code. This thesis favours a repository on the basis of a P2P overlay network. This can overcome typical issues of server-based solutions, such as exposing a single point of failure, scalability, and administrative effort. Furthermore, in a P2P infrastructure server nodes can also be integrated if appropriate. A decentralised implementation repository requires only P2P support for keyword search.

The implementation repository itself is updated by multiple *code providers*. These are entities that provide implementation code themselves and publish metadata descriptions about the implementation code.

Basic Data Structures of the Implementation Repository Using the aforementioned set of description properties allows selecting the best-fitting implementation code. Therefore, all data about available implementations is published as metadata descriptions in the scope of the implementation repository. To avoid duplicated information and to improve extensibility, these descriptions should be modularised into four kinds of metadata.

An *interface description* contains the fully-qualified name of the interface and the interface itself in an abstract manner (e.g., with IDL or WSDL). Within the description, interfaces and complex data types in use are also referenced by their fully-qualified names. This allows dynamic lookup of unknown interfaces and data types.

An *extended functional description* specifies all functional and non-functional implementation-independent properties. These are properties that can be provided by various implementations and therefore are used for selecting a particular implementation out of similar implementations providing the same interface.

An *implementation description* describes a concrete implementation and its compatibility requirements. It includes a reference to the location of the code and a description of the initially accessed implementation element. For instance, in the context of Java this would be the class name of a factory.

Last, a *dependency description* describes dependencies on other functionality and specific implementations. This can be specified by referencing the interface and the implementation description, respectively.

Basic Workflow of Publication, Selection and Loading of Code Before publishing an implementation, a code provider has to generate appropriate metadata, i.e., the interface description, the extended functional description (referencing the interface description), the implementation description (referencing the extended functional description and the concrete implementation) and the dependency description. These metadata descriptions are published via the decentralised code repository. Additionally, the concrete implementation code has to be published, if it is not already served via a separate service.

If an application requires locally unavailable functionality, it passes the fully-qualified name of the required interface with an optional specification of the desired extended functional properties to a dynamic loader entity. This dynamic loader requests the implementation repository to look up the interface description (if the needed functionality is not available, an exception is returned to the calling application). Then, the repository is queried for extended functional descriptions supporting the requested interface. If available, an ordered list of appropriate extended functional descriptions starting with the best-fitting one is returned. On the basis of this list, the dynamic loader queries the repository for implementation descriptions. These should be evaluated with respect to a policy, such as the first-fitting or the best-fitting implementation being selected. Finally, the referenced code has to be loaded.

In case of functional and implementation dependencies the dynamic loader is used again to load the required implementations as per description.

4.1.3.2 JXTA and Dynamic Management of Code

This section gives a brief introduction to the JXTA platform and presents the JXTA built-in facility for dynamic management of code.

JXTA Overview JXTA is a generic P2P platform [Gon01]. It specifies programming-language–independent protocols for fundamental P2P functions, such as storing and retrieving data.

JXTA nodes are called *peers* and implement a super peer infrastructure: standard peers are called *edge peers* and super peers are called *rendezvous peers* managing a set of edge peers. Independent from the peer type, peers are organised in *peer groups*. All JXTA resources, such as peers and peer groups, are uniquely identified and represented by *advertisements* (i.e., XML metadata structures for describing resources). Advertisements are used for resource publication and discovery. JXTA introduces *pipes* as communication channels for providing an abstraction from the underlying physical network infrastructure.

JXTA is a platform-independent specification. For instance, there are interoperable implementations for standard Java, Java ME, C, Perl, Python and Ruby.

Dynamic Lookup and Loading of Services JXTA provides a *generic module framework* for supporting the dynamic integration of JXTA services (i.e., modules) on the basis of code loading. For this purpose, a set of advertisements is introduced. A *module class advertisement* announces the existence of a module and thus provides an abstraction from the class of provided functionality. This advertisement is referenced by a *module specification advertisement* specifying different module versions, which is itself referenced by a *module implementation advertisement* providing implementation-specific details such as the code location.

JXTA already allows building a decentralised module taxonomy to support the discovery and loading of services. Yet, module class advertisements only announce the availability of a general category of functionality. This gives application developers an idea of a particular module specification and supports the selection process at a very high level but for an automated module selection process at application level, additional conventions have to be established. Therefore, the Java reference implementation of JXTA makes implicit assumptions that a module implementation provides a certain interface for starting and stopping a module. However, this is neither specified by the JXTA protocol specification nor declared within advertisements. Additionally, JXTA offers no support for determining and specifying the interface of a module being offered to higher layers, such as an application. This makes it difficult to provide multiple implementations supporting the same protocol and platform but providing different properties. Furthermore, module implementation advertisements should allow the provisioning of compatibility information but this is not standardised so far. This results in JXTA implementations specifying their own format and parameters, which prevents the use of module implementations in context of different JXTA implementations.

To sum up, the JXTA support for dynamic loading and integration of services leads to platform-specific implementations and does not support automatic management of arbitrary code.

4.1.3.3 A JXTA-based Infrastructure for Decentralised Dynamic Management of Code

Although the JXTA approach for dynamic management of code seems to be generic and flexible, the prior section outlined its weaknesses and shortcomings. Thus, it cannot be used as a generic and platform-independent infrastructure for dynamic code management. This section introduces a novel JXTA-based infrastructure for dynamic code management on the basis of the presented generic concept (see Section 4.1.3.1).

Advertisements for dynamic code management This thesis introduces novel advertisements conforming to the specified requirements in Section 4.1.3.1 to provide a custom code management infrastructure on top of JXTA. Figure 4.4 shows the novel advertisement types and their relations. Resources are published by three advertisements in a specific JXTA *code peer group*. JXTA advertisements have a Universally Unique Identifier (UUID) and are able to reference each other using these identifiers.

With respect to Section 4.1.3.1, the basic data structures of the implementation repository are mapped to the corresponding advertisements. An *interface description advertisement* (IDA) announces the mere existence of an interface (e.g., HTTP service interface; see Section 4.1.2) and can be searched using a fully-qualified interface name or keywords. It contains a section with advised criteria, which recommend optional and mandatory functional and non-functional

4.1 Dynamic Management of Code

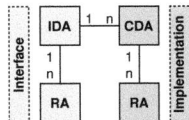

Figure 4.4: Relations of DCM JXTA advertisements

properties for describing a specific implementation (see Section 4.1.2). The interface description is not part of the IDA. It is described in one or more referenced *resource advertisements* (RAs), which represent an arbitrary resource. IDA-referencing *code description advertisements* (CDAs) describe implementations of an interface for a specific platform with the extended functional description containing functional as well non-functional properties, such as the resource demand (e.g., an HTTP service with low resource demand). The CDA references RAs, which contain the implementation description with metadata for loading and instantiating the resource as well as implementation properties, such as size, filename and checksum.

Decentralised Implementation Repository JXTA already provides a standard discovery service, which allows searching for and publishing of arbitrary advertisements. Yet, it supports only search requests with *one* key-value pair as search criteria. Thus, it is impossible to search for advertisements with multiple functional and non-functional properties at the same time. To overcome this issue a query could be executed with only one key-value pair and incompatible advertisements could be filtered out on the requesting peer side. However, this would lead to a high processing load on the requesting side as well as high network load. Hence, an extended *JXTA code discovery service* was developed as part of this thesis. This service allows discovering advertisements with arbitrary criteria. Thus, incompatible advertisements are already sorted out at the resource-providing peers.

For loading and provisioning of code resources a *code sharing service* was developed. This service is able to automatically create an RA with the concrete loading address for a given resource (the IDA as well as the CDA has to be provided by the developer). The service manages physical resource provisioning as well. In the prototype, a simple HTTP-based *resource provider* was implemented; here, the service automatically starts a Web server serving the provided resource. The service supports resource loading as well. Therefore, an RA has to be passed to the service. The transfer method is dynamically selected on the basis of the RA data. Specific *transfer handlers* implement the particular mechanism and can be loaded on demand as well. There is a JXTA-based handler as a basis. It enables seamless data transfer across firewalls and using a

4 Infrastructure Services for Mobile and Ubiquitous Computing Environments

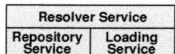

Figure 4.5: Dynamic code management services

Bluetooth connection for data transfer due to JXTA-provided transparency.

Dynamic Code Management Services The DCM platform consists of three services (see Figure 4.5). The *loading service* supports publication as well as automatic selection and loading of implementation code on the basis of the aforementioned JXTA services. The *repository service* manages and provides already loaded and locally available resources. With the help of these services, the *resolver service* allows automatic code dependency resolution.

The loading service enables dynamic integration of implementation code. Figure 4.6 shows an exemplary selection process for an HTTP service implementation with optional support for dynamic content and maximal throughput with respect to the available implementations. Therefore, the loading service expects either an interface or an implementation name as input. Additionally, functional and non-functional properties specify the required resource. There are mandatory and optional properties. Mandatory properties build the basis for the selection of compatible implementation code. Optional properties are used for rating all compatible implementations that have been found.

Searching for code resources is implemented with the aforementioned JXTA code discovery service. An important factor is the time period the loading service waits for incoming advertisements. Due to the fact that this is highly application- and environment-dependent, the code discovery service allows the specification of a timeout as well as a threshold for incoming advertisements after which the selection process can start.

The evaluation of found resources is implemented by a comparison of the metadata of corresponding CDAs and finally results in an implementation ranking on the basis of scores. Therefore, optional properties have a quantifier that is defined by the implementation developer and represents a relative importance of the requirement (throughput has a quantifier of 40 and support for dynamic content has a quantifier of 50 in Figure 4.6). These quantifiers can also be overwritten by runtime parameters in order to allow a user-defined discovery. The loading service provides a set of *type handlers*, which are used for comparing particular non-functional demands with non-functional properties of a specific CDA. These properties have specific types, for instance, *string* or *version*. The corresponding type handler allows a comparison of the typed properties. Whenever a specific type handler is unavailable it can be loaded dynamically using the DCM

4.1 Dynamic Management of Code

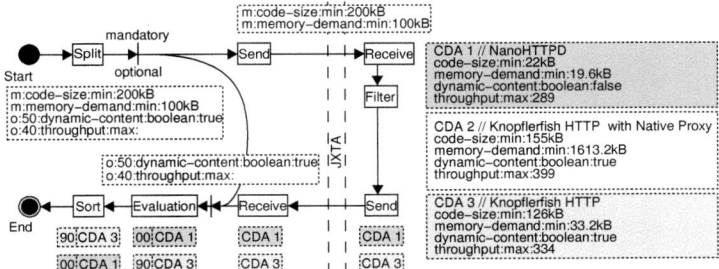

Figure 4.6: Dynamic code selection process for an HTTP service

infrastructure (type handlers are implementation code as well). If a CDA fulfils an optional demand, the corresponding score is assigned to it. Scores are added if further optional properties are met (in Figure 4.6 CDA 3 is ranked highest because it supports maximal throughput and dynamic content). For an improved evaluation min/max type handlers were developed as well. These credit the full score to the best-fitting CDA, a null-score to the worst-fitting one and a continuous value for those in between (e.g., required for the maximal throughput property). Finally, the best ranked resource is loaded using the corresponding RA.

The repository service manages already loaded and locally available resources. In order to save time and network resources, applications are able to search for cached implementations at the local repository service first. Subsequently, the loading service can be used to search for remote implementations using JXTA.

The loading service and the repository service build the basis for providing the resolver service, which enables automatic code dependency resolution of resources that were loaded. Therefore, the resolver service reads dependencies from a special *resolve descriptor*. The resolve descriptor contains the interface name (prefixed by byIDA) as well as mandatory and optional functional and non-functional demands (see Figure 4.7). These demands can be separated into sections, which implement a namespace. Optional demands are prefixed with 'o' and have a score, while mandatory demands are prefixed by 'm'. A dependency on a specific implementation leads to a specific byCDA section within the resolve descriptor. Again, it defines functional and non-functional demands of the specific implementation. Dependency resolution is achieved by first[4] querying the repository service for implementations being already locally available. If no appropriate

---
[4]The search method order is configurable in the prototype.

```
1  byIDA:org.osgi.service.http.HttpService: {
2    compatibility {
3      m:os.name:String:windows
4      m:lang.name:String:java
5      m:code−size:min:200kB
6      m:memory−demand:min:100kB
7    }
8    properties {
9      o:50:dynamic−content:boolean:true
10     o:40:throughput:max:
11   }
12 }
```

Figure 4.7: Resolve descriptor with IDA dependency

implementation is found, the loading service is used to search for best-fitting implementations. In case of functional dependencies, the loading service starts with searching for IDAs with the required interface name, whereas for specific implementation dependencies the service starts with searching for CDAs with the needed implementation name.

4.1.4 Dynamic Management of Platform-specific Code with OSGi

As already mentioned, OSGi emerged as a de-facto standard for modularising and managing all kinds of complex Java-based software. With *Concierge*, OSGi is available on typical devices for mobile and UbiComp scenarios. Thus, in addition to the platform-independent prototype on the basis of JXTA, this thesis integrates the generic DCM approach into OSGi as well. Figure 4.8 shows the architecture. The JXTA P2P services for the decentralised implementation repository and the dynamic code management services, which were presented in Section 4.1.3.3, are provided as OSGi bundles. The following paragraphs introduce OSGi and the particular integration efforts with an enhanced OSGi bundle definition. Then, Section 4.1.4.6 presents an integration of the novel OSGi DCM service with AWSM.

4.1.4.1 OSGi

OSGi is an open and standardised service platform defined by the OSGi Alliance [OSG07a]. The platform provides a lean Java-based component framework, which allows the installation, update and uninstallation of components at runtime. Components are standard Java archives

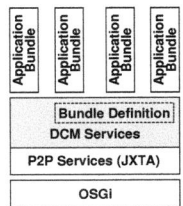

Figure 4.8: DCM architecture for OSGi

with a special manifest containing metadata. Such components are called *bundles* and can contain libraries and applications in terms of OSGi *services*. These services implement a regular Java interface and are registered with this interface name and optional metadata at an OSGi platform *service registry*. Bundles are able to share functionality on the basis of Java packages that can be exported and imported. The coordination of such bundle dependencies is part of the OSGi framework.

Following the idea of the service-oriented architecture [Bar03], OSGi services can be built on basis of other bundles' services. Due to the fact that OSGi was originally designed with focus on local applications, such as gateways and set-top boxes, the OSGi framework provides functions for *local* service discovery and instantiation. Thus, services are able to collaborate only within the OSGi system's frontiers. Automatic service dependency resolution with remote service repositories is not part of the OSGi specification, but services have to be installed locally by an administrator[5]. Dependencies can in fact be described with the bundle manifest header Import-Service but the actual resolution of service dependencies is left to bundle developers even in the local case. Therefore, OSGi provides support for monitoring the availability of local services. Since OSGi release 4, there is a declarative services specification [OSG07b]. It provides an automatic approach for service dependency resolution. Yet, it is restricted to a *local* OSGi framework. Up to now, only few OSGi framework implementations, such as Eclipse Equinox [Ecl09c], provide an implementation.

---

[5]OSGi release 4.2 [OSG09] that has just been approved in September 2009 contains a *remote services* specification but there is no implementation so far.

```
 1  Name: org.knopflerfish.bundle.http.HttpServiceImpl
 2  Version: 1.3
 3  Interface : org.osgi.service.http.HttpService
 4  InterfaceVersion : 1.0
 5  InternalName: knopf_http_1_3
 6  compatibility {
 7    os.name:String:linux
 8    os.version:version :[2.4;2.6)
 9  }
10  properties {
11
12    code-size:min:155kB
13    memory-demand:min:1613.2kB
14    dynamic-content:boolean:true
15    throughput:max:399
16  }
```

Figure 4.9: Exemplary code description manifest

4.1.4.2 Extended Bundle Description

In addition to the standard OSGi bundle manifest [OSG07a], further manifests were added by the author to describe bundles with respect to the DCM platform. These manifests allow automatic JXTA advertisement generation in the loading service (i.e., IDA and CDA) and bundle dependency specification. They are ignored by OSGi framework implementations that are not aware of the DCM platform.

Interface description manifests describe the service interfaces within a bundle and are used for IDA generation and respective *code description manifests* contain information for CDA generation. Figure 4.9 shows an exemplary code description manifest that describes an HTTP bundle for Linux version equal to or greater 2.4 and less than 2.6 providing an HTTP service with support for dynamic content.

The standard OSGi bundle manifest header **Import-Service** is used to specify service dependencies. As already mentioned, a *resolve descriptor* is introduced for specifying dependencies on other bundles with functional and non-functional demands (see Figure 4.7). There, the interface name within the **Import-Service** header maps to the interface name within the resolve descriptor (prefixed by **byIDA**). A **Require-Bundle** header describes a bundle dependency and thus results in searching for a specific implementation described by a CDA (see Figure 4.10 for

4.1 Dynamic Management of Code

```
1  Bundle-SymbolicName:
2              org.knopflerfish.bundle.http.HttpServiceImpl
3  Bundle-Version: 1.3
4  Bundle-Name: HTTP service bundle
5  Bundle-Activator: org.knopflerfish.bundle.http.Activator
6  Require-Bundle: org.knopflerfish.bundle.http.impl.HTTPBase
7  Import-Package: org.knopflerfish.bundle.http.impl.util,
8              org.knopflerfish.bundle.http.impl.tools
```

Figure 4.10: Bundle manifest with dependency on HTTPBase bundle

a bundle manifest describing a dependency on an HTTPBase bundle providing shared HTTP functionality).

4.1.4.3 Manual start of loading process: OSGi console

Most OSGi frameworks provide a management console (e.g., for manual bundle installation and starting). DCM was seamlessly integrated into the OSGi console of Apache Felix [Apa09a] and Eclipse Equinox [Ecl09c] as a part of this thesis. For resolving the dependencies of an installed bundle the command `DCM_resolve <bundle_id>` is used (`bundle_id` identifies the bundle to be resolved). Internally, the resolver service manages dependency resolution (see Section 4.1.3.3). There is also a basic backtracking mechanism: if dependencies of dependent bundles cannot be resolved, an alternative from the previous selection is tried. For installation with automatic resolving of bundle dependencies `DCM_install <url>` is used (`url` specifies the bundle file location).

4.1.4.4 Automatic start of loading process: Service Tracker

For seamless deployment of locally unavailable services a standard OSGi service tracker [OSG07a] is used. This enables a completely automated process of selection, loading and installation of the best-fitting bundle and services without user interaction.

In general, a service tracker decouples OSGi bundles from directly monitoring whether required services are available at runtime. For this purpose, a service tracker autonomously observes service registration and deregistration activities within the OSGi framework. This capability allows resolving required services with the service tracker. Therefore, the service tracker expects filter criteria, such as the service name and service vendor in terms of an LDAP string [OSG07a].

4 Infrastructure Services for Mobile and Ubiquitous Computing Environments

These filter criteria enable determining a specific implementation in case of multiple suitable ones. Some filter criteria are proposed by the OSGi specification but user-defined criteria are left open to developers. Parameters within the LDAP strings are matched against *service properties*, which can be specified at service registration. A timeout can be specified for the case that a required service is unavailable.

Within the scope of this thesis, an existing service tracker implementation was extended to automatically deploy bundles, which implement a required service according to user-defined requirements. In general, this enables bundle developers who use a traditional service tracker to implement a blueprint of a service-based application (i.e., an application construction plan on the basis of an initial service with all required bundle and service dependencies that build up the whole application) without caring about local availability of the needed services; node-tailored services are automatically deployed by the novel service tracker. The OSGi-compliant service tracker enables a seamless integration of service-containing bundles without any OSGi framework modifications. Therefore, it uses the aforementioned dynamic code management services (see Section 4.1.3.3). The preferred method order (i.e., use local bundle or always load the bundle with the DCM platform) is specified as an ordered tuple within the LDAP string. If no such policy is specified, first locally available bundles are used. Then, if appropriate local bundles are unavailable the DCM platform is used.

To seamlessly integrate the DCM platform within the service tracker, given LDAP filter criteria specifying non-functional requirements are automatically mapped to the DCM platform for performing queries for bundles providing the needed services. For this purpose, the LDAP string is parsed and non-functional requirements, which are intended for the DCM platform, are automatically extracted (these are prefixed by `dcm`). Then, an OSGi-local query is performed for determining whether an appropriate implementation for the requested service is already available. Potential service candidates are matched against the given non-functional requirements and the best-fitting one is returned. If no adequate service implementation is found, the service tracker uses the DCM platform (see Section 4.1.3.3). Therefore, a resolve descriptor is generated for the service interface and the given non-functional requirements are inserted as mandatory and optional items. For avoiding network traffic, the repository service queries its local cache for bundles containing appropriate service implementations. If no such bundles are available the loading service is used. A suitable bundle satisfying at least the mandatory requirements is automatically discovered, selected, downloaded, and installed. In case of service and bundle dependencies, the resolver service attempts to resolve these dependencies with the DCM services as already described. A basic backtracking mechanism is started if dependent bundles cannot be resolved (see previous section). If all dependencies are successfully resolved, the bundles can

4.1 Dynamic Management of Code

Bundle Size	Platform	Deployment Time (s)		
		LAN Local Network	WAN Inter-University	Internet
0.1 MB	DCM	1.55 ± 0.10	1.55 ± 0.07	1.55 ± 0.06
	OBR	0.42 ± 0.10	0.48 ± 0.05	0.49 ± 0.05
1 MB	DCM	1.90 ± 0.05	2.31 ± 0.10	4.80 ± 0.24
	OBR	0.56 ± 0.05	0.64 ± 0.06	3.01 ± 0.17
10 MB	DCM	6.81 ± 0.08	11.42 ± 0.22	33.80 ± 0.26
	OBR	3.31 ± 0.09	3.32 ± 0.12	24.74 ± 0.21

Figure 4.11: Evaluation of bundle loading time with DCM vs. OBR

be started. When starting bundles, their new services are registered and the OSGi framework propagates *service events*. The service tracker listens for these events and manages references of all appropriate service candidates matching the non-functional requirements.

For preventing the OSGi framework from locking during DCM network operations, the novel service tracker performs remote queries, downloading and bundle installation within a separate thread. Consequently, service queries can be repeated continuously by the service tracker until an appropriate service implementation is available without affecting the OSGi framework operation.

4.1.4.5 Evaluation: Dynamic Code Management vs. OSGi Bundle Repository

This thesis evaluates DCM on the basis of JXTA 2.4.1 in comparison to the server-based OSGi Bundle Repository (OBR) to determine the overhead of the decentralised approach in contrast to a pure server-based solution. The OBR provides a central Web server with an XML file describing bundles that can be downloaded on demand. A typical scenario of the measurement case would be the dynamic loading of an application on demand. Therefore, the application developer has to specify some kind of application construction plan in terms of bundle and service dependencies. These dependencies can be resolved either automatically using the DCM platform or manually with the OBR.

For the evaluation, an OSGi bundle was implemented, which requests a locally unavailable bundle at startup time. It measures the time to load, install and start the requested bundle. For the loading process either DCM or the OBR is used. Due to the fact that the OBR automatically loads the first available bundle implementation, DCM is also configured to select the first-fitting bundle in order to obtain comparable results. The OBR client parses an XML description of the repository at startup time and thus does not support repository changes at runtime. To allow dynamic changes at runtime, this XML file has to be parsed each time before the discovery process. Thus, this time is taken into account for the OBR performance cases to make it comparable to the DCM approach. Both systems, an DCM-providing node as well as the OBR, are running on the same machine during the measurements. The bundle size was diversified to estimate the overhead of the JXTA-based code management infrastructure. The loading process is evaluated for different network configurations. Figure 4.11 shows the loading time of a particular bundle with the loading-client and the particular infrastructure being in the same *local network* (switched 100Mbit LAN), in different but *inter-university*-connected networks (fast WAN connection between University of Erlangen and Ulm University) and in different *Internet-connected* networks (6Mbit DSL WAN). The experiment was repeated 20 times and the average deployment time was calculated with the standard deviation. Apache Felix 1.0.0 running on Sun Java 1.6.0_03 was used as evaluation platform. An AMD Athlon 64 2.20GHz processor with 1GB RAM acted as client machine, while an Intel XEON 2.40GHz processor with 2GB RAM acted as server machine hosting either the OBR or the DCM platform.

For the performance evaluation in the local network, the OBR outperforms the DCM platform. However, while for a 0.1 MB bundle OBR is factor 3.69 faster than DCM, the factor shrinks[6] to 2.05 for a 10 MB sized bundle. Performance in the inter-university WAN scenario is similar to the local network scenario. Although the DCM results show that the JXTA data transfer does not scale well, bundle sizes greater than 1 MB are rather uncommon for OSGi. The Internet WAN scenario is similar to the previous performance cases. However, it shows the great potential of DCM: while the probability of a local-network–connected OBR repository is quite low, the probability of another DCM code sharing peer within the same local network having already cached a needed bundle is higher (e.g., a team working in the same department probably needs the same software; thus, the probability is high that a local team member already shares a required update). This can drastically decrease deployment time due to loading from a local-network–connected node instead of an Internet-connected one (OBR Internet WAN deployment times vs. DCM LAN deployment time).

Additionally, DCM solves some issues of the OBR. For instance, OBR does not support non-functional properties during the discovery and selection process. Moreover, it automatically selects the first only functionally fitting bundle. OBR is a pure server-based solution with its well-known limitations, such as scalability (the performance evaluation was made with a very small bundle repository providing only 10 bundles; in case of a bigger one, a longer XML file would have

---

[6] Discovery time is independent of the bundle size, whereas the transfer time increases accordingly. Thus, with an increasing bundle size, discovery time becomes insignificant.

4.1 Dynamic Management of Code

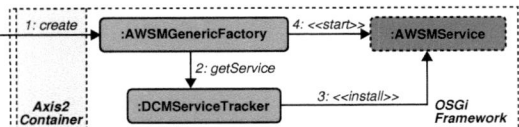

Figure 4.12: Integration of DCM with AWSM

to be loaded and parsed). The P2P approach enables each OSGi system running DCM to share bundles, which reduces administrative efforts to a minimum. Moreover, DCM is independent of the data transfer mechanism (OBR is restricted to HTTP). For the measurements, the JXTA-based data handler was used, which provides the ability to transfer data across firewalls and via Bluetooth. Last but not least, using the OBR forces manual bundle selection, while DCM allows transparent service instantiation (see Section 4.1.4.4). Thus, considering the issues that were solved in comparison to the OBR, the overhead of the DCM platform is adequate. Especially in the case that a local DCM system already loaded a needed bundle the overhead of the P2P approach is low or it performs even better than the OBR.

4.1.4.6 Integration with AWSM

Due to its excellent support for modularised Java software, OSGi is a good candidate to modularise *AWSM service* facets (this way, fundamental *AWSM service* adaptation as introduced in Section 3.3.2 can be implemented with bundle reconfiguration). As a proof-of-concept, the author developed a prototypical integration of DCM on the basis of OSGi with AWSM. It is possible to run Axis2 on top of OSGi. Therefore, standard OSGi bundles have to be extended by a `services.xml` description, which specifies the OSGi services to expose as Axis Web services [AE08].

Figure 4.12 shows the approach to integrate AWSM into an OSGi environment running DCM. For this purpose, a generic factory is implemented as an OSGi service, which is remotely accessible as an Axis SOAP Web service. The factory implements the generic factory interface as specified in Section 3.3.2.2 (thus, it is externally not recognisable as an OSGi service) and uses the DCM service tracker to install the required target Web service facet (see Figure 4.12, step 3). If the code is not available, the service tracker tries to install the target service as described in Section 4.1.4.4. If the installation is successful, the service is started with the standard OSGi command. AWSM services that are implemented as OSGi services include a `services.xml` file, which specifies the Web service to expose. Thus, after installation, the provided OSGi service automatically registers itself as a SOAP Web service to Axis to implement the desired target Web service facet.

4.1.5 Basic Security Considerations

This section discusses security risks that may arise when using the DCM platform. These are first split into network and local risks. Then, possible solutions are provided.

Network Risks In general, JXTA is an open P2P infrastructure, in which any JXTA peer may join and leave the network. However, peers may behave maliciously and thus compromise the network. JXTA provides the concept of secure peer groups for this purpose. There, only peers that provide pre-negotiated credentials are able to join such a group. This establishes trust between peers [The07a].

JXTA messages are plain XML files. This enables peers—especially rendezvous peers—modifying these messages without notice of any other peer. A solution to this would be using standard XML signatures [Net02]. Additionally, peers may intercept bundle code transfer. Especially when transferring confidential data, such as bundles developers have to pay for, this is a serious concern. A solution would be the development of a transfer handler using transport layer security (TLS). JXTA XML messages could be secured using XML encryption [W3C02].

Another issue are rendezvous peer crashes. This leads to unreachable subnets. An effective solution could be implemented within the subnets. There, peers have to monitor the rendezvous peer. In case of a crash, any edge peer within the subnet becomes a rendezvous peer (JXTA provides basic mechanisms to implement such behaviour).

Local Risks A serious problem with dynamic code loading is malicious code. Due to the fact that both prototypes (i.e., standalone JXTA and OSGi) are Java-based they provide standard Java security mechanisms, such as sandboxing [WLAG93]. OSGi provides additional support for digital code signatures [Nec97] and a special optional *Permission Admin* service for a fine-grained security-related framework configuration since release 4 [OSG07a].

4.2 Generic Context Service

As already mentioned, the increase of mobile and interconnected devices demands for equally ubiquitous and mobile applications. Due to the heterogeneity of devices, applications have to adapt to the environment they are executed in (e.g., on the basis of the AXM pattern; see Chapter 3). This requires context management in the environment and context-sensitivity of the application.

This section introduces a novel generic context service with a generic context model. The context service has a modular architecture and provides context collection, discovery and monitoring. It is generic in the sense that it offers extension points for integrating future context domains and provides a Web service interface for standard-compliant interaction in heterogeneous environments. After briefly considering security, the section shows the integration of the prototype into the AWSM platform, which provides fundamental adaptivity to applications (see Section 3.3.2). As a use case, the implementation of the novel mobile media player application (see Section 2.2.2) is described in detail with respect to the implementation of context awareness.

4.2.1 Background

This section first defines context as it is used in this work. Then it presents the current state-of-the-art with respect to context modelling approaches.

4.2.1.1 Context

Context is known in several scientific fields such as linguistics, psychology and computer science. This work focuses on definitions used in the latter. Besides low-level definitions of context such as the process context used with multitasking, there are also high-level definitions. For the first time, *Schilit et al.* [SAW94] define context as a set of three aspects: *Where are you? Who are you with? What resources are nearby?* Dey [Dey01] criticises that it is impossible to define context by naming all of its components because these are highly situation dependent. Additionally, he disagrees with the limitation to the user perspective and thus gives an own definition describing context as *any information that can be used to characterise the situation of an entity* (i.e., person, place or object relevant to the user-application interaction). Due to the fact that Dey's definition is a very generic approach, it is used in this thesis to define the requirements of the generic context model.

4.2.1.2 Context Modelling

The number of sensors in modern devices is constantly increasing. This allows fine-grained descriptions of the application environment. However, standardised context modelling and distribution are required for interoperability.

There are several approaches to model context, which mainly differ in complexity of syntax and expressiveness. For instance, *Schilit et al.* [SAW94] use key-value-pairs to store context information. Yet, key-value-pairs are a very limited approach as they do not support hierarchies/namespaces for separating identically named properties of different context components.

Graphical models, for instance on the basis of Object Role Modelling (ORM) are amongst others used by *Henricksen et al.* [HIR03]. They use them in the design phase of context modelling and for defining schemas to store context into relational databases. However, this approach is neither processible nor reasonable for small mobile devices.

Further modelling approaches use object-orientation, markup languages and ontologies. There is no clear separation between these approaches, for instance, *Composite Capability/Preference Profiles* (CC/PP) [W3C07a] for describing device specifications and user preferences are expressed with the Resource Description Framework (RDF) [W3C04b]. RDF is an XML application, which can be used to define ontologies by building a graph with interlinked nodes representing resources. The edges of an RDF graph describe relations between resources. OWL [W3C04a] is built on top of RDF to create a more expressive ontology language. Adding object-oriented language concepts, such as classes and inheritance, OWL allows modelling complex relations between entities. For instance, *Strang et al.* [SLPF03] use OWL in a context model to allow contextual service discovery. Due to its sophisticated features, the high expressiveness and the use of XML, OWL is an excellent candidate for modelling context in a generic way.

4.2.2 Related Work

Context provisioning is a very popular research area. The following paragraphs give a broad overview by describing possible approaches with particular realisations.

For instance, *Schmidt et al.* [SAT+99] describe a system generating events when entering/leaving certain situations. For gathering characteristic context information about such situations, physical and logical sensors are used. These either detect physical values, such as brightness and temperature or logical values belonging to a specific device such as available bandwidth and the currently connected GSM cell. Both types of values are processed and unified in a higher layer called *cues* to derive higher level context descriptions. Due to a multi-tier architecture, sensors can be flexibly added to support further context components. However, there is no insight on how to model context and due to the missing documentation of the system interface, the usability remains unclear. The most severe limitation is the missing support of context distribution. This is essential to share context information between different components within a UbiComp platform.

Dey et al. [DAS99] create a context environment as a basis for several UbiComp applications, such as indoor-navigation and location-based messaging. The environment is aware of context, such as nearby persons, and provides applications with events at context changes. The authors use the concept of widgets known from GUIs to encapsulate sensor-specific drivers and protocols. These *context widgets* can be linked among each other and thereby build up complex context descriptions. For separating application logic from context processing, *context interpreters* aggregate widgets. Applications obtain context information using a centralised *context server*. All components can run on different devices and thus be distributed. The context information is modelled with XML and spread with a proprietary protocol. Thus, in contrast to standard protocols, such as Web services, developers cannot use code generators to create communication stubs. Moreover, there is no support for query languages to specify required context profiles.

Indulska et al. [IRRH03] describe how to build context-aware systems on top of CC/PP. They identify context detection, interpretation and management as main challenges. The authors propose a three-tier architecture with *awareness modules* to abstract from sensors/actors, a *context manager* to manage aggregated context information in a context repository and a context-aware application layer. Applications are able to subscribe to notifications on context changes. Although context modelling with CC/PP elements allows reusing an existing ontology, it is heavily limited to a concrete application domain (i.e., describing capabilities of mobile devices).

Da Rocha and Endler [dRE06] present an approach for context management in UbiComp environments. Yet, in contrast to the system proposed in this thesis, they use object-oriented context modelling. This requires a proprietary infrastructure supporting context operations, such as **store** and **query**. Unlike the approach of this thesis, they assume the context service and the infrastructure being built upon the same middleware. The approach of this thesis supports heterogeneity by building only on standards, such as Web services and OWL.

There are context services, which are—in contrast to the generic approach of this thesis—restricted to single context components. For instance, *Ranganathan et al.* [RAMC$^+$04] developed a context service for location awareness in UbiComp environments.

4.2.3 Requirements

The following sections define requirements for a generic context model and management. These serve as a guideline for designing and implementing the novel context service as part of this thesis.

4.2.3.1 Context Model

Due to the fact that the context model should suit a generic context service in terms of supporting as many applications as possible, the most important requirement is the extensibility of the context model to abstract from a concrete application domain. Therefore, it should provide an initial ontology, which allows adding further context components. For reusing existing context components the modelling language should support some kind of inheritance. Additionally, it is desirable to model equivalence relations between properties that are named differently but share the same semantics.

A further requirement is support for decentralised modelling. Developers should be able to compose ontologies from different sources. Sources should include publicly available context components and individual domain-specific ones.

The chosen modelling language should be supported by an application programming interface (API) in the most relevant programming languages. This eases context processing inside the context service. Furthermore, ensuring compatible data types through all layers of the context service calls for a type system. Due to the fact that context analysis is the basis of context discovery and monitoring, the modelling language should provide a corresponding querying language. Both languages should be accepted standards in order to ensure future interoperability.

4.2.3.2 Context Management

Context management should aggregate information from multiple distributed context services. For immediately reflecting changes in dynamic parts of the environment the knowledge base should be continuously updated. In order to allow context discovery, the knowledge base should provide a public interface using standard protocols. Such an interface should accept complex queries, which define context profiles (e.g., requested by mobile applications for initiating migration). Then, this query should be executed by the knowledge base for discovering the requested context.

4.2 Generic Context Service

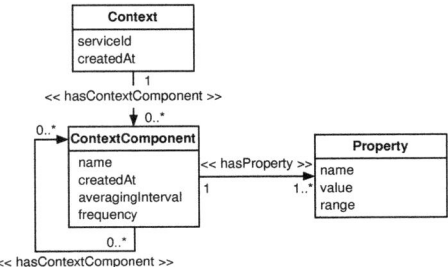

Figure 4.13: Context model structure

In addition to the public interface, there should be an event mechanism that allows informing about context changes. Detecting required context violations enables applications reacting autonomously at runtime.

4.2.4 Context Service

This section first presents the generic context model of the context service. Then, it shows the architecture and describes the approach for context management.

4.2.4.1 Context Model

Figure 4.13 shows the structure of the context model. Each context has a `serviceId` defining its scope to correlate context to physical objects (e.g., regarding AWSM, the id allows the factory finder to correlate context to particular factories; see Section 4.2.6). The property `createdAt` contains the creation time, which can be used for implementing caching strategies for context discovery. A context consists of multiple context components. These components represent topics such as *network, audio, video* and *user*. Such a context component consists of properties (with name, value and possible value range), further context components or both. The properties `averagingInterval` (interval of values being considered for averaging) and `frequency` can be used to measure the continuousness of context components (could be referenced within a context query).

4 Infrastructure Services for Mobile and Ubiquitous Computing Environments

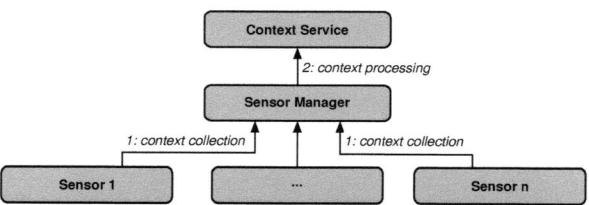

Figure 4.14: Context service architecture

According to the evaluation of modelling approaches in Section 4.2.1.2, the model is realised with standard OWL (i.e., *OWL Lite* [W3C04a]). This allows using the standard query language SPARQL. Extensibility is achieved with OWL inheritance mechanisms using the RDF schema element `rdfs:subClassOf`. Value ranges and equivalency relations are specified with `rdfs:range` and `owl:equivalentProperty` elements.

4.2.4.2 Architecture

Figure 4.14 shows the service architecture, which is divided into three layers to separate the functional aspects of context sensing, collection and processing (e.g., proposed by *Dey et al.* [DAS99] and *Coutaz et al.* [CR02]).

At the lowest layer, *sensors* (i.e., virtual sensors) collect context data. Each sensor belongs to exactly one context component (see Figure 4.13). This eases the extensibility of the context model.

A sensor is able to collect information from different sources, such as static configuration files, individual detection methods and user interaction. Static context information can be provided in XML configuration files. These documents contain key-value-pairs allowing sensors to parse context information. Keys are the URIs within the context ontology, which uniquely identify context component properties. Unlike static information, dynamic information needs continuous detection at runtime. Corresponding detection methods have to be implemented individually. Yet, there is a basic naming convention: a detection method for property `x` is named `detectX()` and must return a value with the appropriate data type being specified in the context ontology. Another alternative for delivering context information to a sensor is user interaction, for instance,

4.2 Generic Context Service

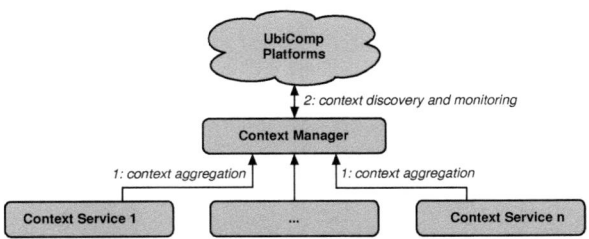

Figure 4.15: Context management

using a GUI (sensors are implemented as Java Management Extensions (JMX) Beans, which makes them accessible for graphical management tools, such as the JConsole [Sun08]).

Depending on the information characteristics, each property value is continuously updated and these continuous values can be averaged using a Gaussian filter. Functionality being shared by all sensors, such as updating and averaging, is located within an abstract sensor class. Thus, developers have to implement only the parts that are related to a particular context component. Additionally, as part of this thesis, an Eclipse plugin was developed, which is able to generate sensor-specific code templates out of OWL context component descriptions.

One layer above, the *sensor manager* is situated. It is able to dynamically instantiate sensors and aggregates their information in a context description (i.e., OWL instance of the context model). The public methods `getContext()` and `getContextComponents()` provide OWL context descriptions according to application needs.

A *context service* makes context publicly available to UbiComp platforms, such as AWSM. It is implemented as a Web service and delegates requests to an internal/configured sensor manager.

4.2.4.3 Context Management

Local context descriptions delivered by context services have to be managed domain-wide to build up a comprehensive knowledge base. Figure 4.15 shows the responsible *context manager* and its relation to context services and UbiComp platforms, such as AWSM.

```
1  PREFIX ctx: <http://domain.com/context#>
2  PREFIX net: <http://domain.com/network#>
3
4  SELECT ?serviceId
5  WHERE {
6    ?context ctx:serviceId ?serviceId ;
7            ctx:hasContextComponent ?network.
8
9    ?network net:upstream ?up;
10           net:downstream ?down.
11
12   FILTER(?up > 1000000 && ?down > 5000000)
13 }
```

Figure 4.16: Sample context query in SPARQL

Context prefetching reduces query response times at the knowledge base. Thus, the context manager periodically requests information from registered context services. This thesis advocates such a pull strategy because it supports resource-limited devices as context services can be implemented as passive entities and thus be as lightweight as possible. Context descriptions are buffered in a context store within the context manager.

The context manager executes search queries using SPARQL. Figure 4.16 shows an exemplary query selecting the **serviceId** of each context that matches a minimum network up- and downstream. The query method of the context manager expects a Boolean parameter specifying whether to query information that is cached or to pull current information from context services.

Context monitoring builds the basis for autonomous behaviour, such as rule-based migration. Thus, the context manager provides a *context monitor* as well. For monitoring particular context, listeners can be registered at the context manager with the monitored context's **serviceId**, the monitored condition and the call-back address (i.e., URL). These registrations are delegated to the context monitor, which periodically checks if the context still meets the given conditions. Once a condition is violated the monitor notifies the corresponding listener by sending a message to its registered call-back address.

4.2.5 Basic Security Considerations

This section provides a basic view on security concerns with respect to the presented design of the context service.

In general, sensors, the sensor manager and the context service should be deployed on the same local node. There, ensuring a secure environment should be a trivial issue. Yet, sensors are implemented on the basis of JMX, which allows remote access to beans [Sun08, Sun06c]. Thus, it is possible that sensors and the sensor manager are deployed on different nodes. In this case, there has to be a trust relationship between both entities. If there was no such relationship, malicious sensors could provide wrong context and unauthorised sensor managers could access private context, respectively. Furthermore, data transfer should be encrypted to avoid eavesdropping (e.g., JMX supports Secure Sockets Layer (SSL)).

Moreover, there has to be a trust relationship between the context services and the aggregating context manager. Under other circumstances, malicious context services could provide wrong context and unauthorised entities acting as a context manager could read private context, respectively. Again, data transfer should be encrypted to prevent other entities from wiretapping. Due to the fact that both services are implemented as Web services, standard Web service data encryption mechanisms on the basis of *WS-Security* can be used [OAS06].

For mobile and UbiComp platforms, such as AWSM, it is a severe issue to ensure a trust relationship with the context manager. Otherwise, malicious context services could falsify decisions made on the basis of discovered context and malicious context managers could wrongly notify about violated context constraints, respectively. For reasons of data confidentiality, data transfer should be encrypted again.

As already described in Section 3.2.4, trust can be implemented with centralised or decentralised infrastructures (i.e., public key infrastructure (PKI) [FS03] and Web of trust [CDF[+]07]). JMX supports X.509 certificates [CSF[+]08] to implement such an approach while *WS-Security* [OAS06] can be used for implementing trust between Web services.

4.2.6 Integration of Context Support into AWSM

This section shows the integration of context support into AWSM. Then, it describes the implementation of the novel mobile media player application (see Section 2.2.2) on the basis of the context-enhanced AWSM platform.

```
1  public interface ContextAwareAWSMService extends AWSMService {
2    public String adapt(String targetFacet, String context, String facFinderURI);
3    public String copy(String targetFacet, String context, String facFinderURI);
4    public String move(String targetFacet, String context, String facFinderURI);
5    public void contextChanged (String condition);
6  }
```

Figure 4.17: `ContextAwareAWSMService` interface (Java)

As already described in Section 3.3.2, the AWSM prototype allows migrating to locations, where a needed facet can be created. In addition to this functional criterion, non-functional criteria (i.e., context) shall be considered during migration target discovery. Thus, the *AWSM service* interface is extended with several life-cycle methods that allow specifying the target context (see Figure 4.17). Such a context profile is specified with SPARQL and thus can internally be used for context discovery without change. However, discovering migration targets is not processed by the *AWSM service* itself but delegated to the factory finder (see below). Another addition to the *AWSM service* interface is necessary to receive notifications about context changes. In this case the method `contextChanged()` is called by the context monitor. The parameter specifies the context condition (i.e., SPARQL query), which enables applications reacting to particular context changes. This behaviour is comparable to standard GUI toolkits, in which events also contain information about their source.

The factory finder (see Section 3.3.2) integrates context-awareness into the factory search. Therefore, factories do not only register supported facets but also the `serviceId` (see Section 4.2.4.1) of the responsible context service (typically colocated on the respective factory's device). The factory finder allows searching for factories, which are able to create a certain facet and are located in a desired context. The context is specified with a SPARQL query and the discovery process is delegated to a known context manager (see Section 4.2.4.3). Appropriate factories are found by determining the intersection of both search results (matching facet *and* context). These factories are returned as a list of factory addresses ordered according to similarity with the requested context (e.g., specific location with minimum CPU).

4.2.6.1 Context-aware Mobile Media Player Application

This section describes the prototypical implementation of the novel mobile media player as a proof-of-concept for the AWSM platform in conjunction with the context service. The media player is able to fundamentally adapt to its environment by automatically migrating for spontaneously using presentation resources in the user's surroundings (see Section 2.2.2).

4.2 Generic Context Service

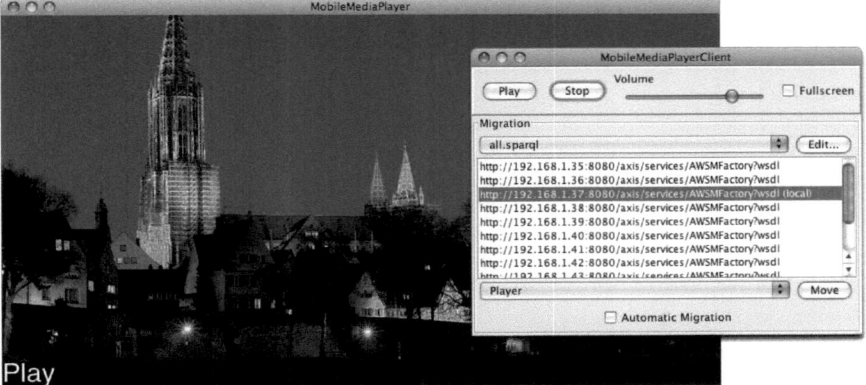

Figure 4.18: Context-aware mobile media player GUI

Today, several manual steps have to be carried out in the following scenario: a person moving around listens to a song on a mobile media player. When this person enters her living room the same song should continue to play on a stationary device. With the AWSM platform, such a mobile media player providing this functionality only has to extend the *AWSM service* implementation. Then, the player can be moved to another device without any user interaction (see Section 3.4.2).

Figure 4.18 shows the media player GUI of the prototype implementation. The client window has two main areas for player control and migration. The top area contains controls that trigger calls to the player Web service. The lower part of the migration panel provides a list of context profiles (i.e., **SPARQL** queries) with different priorities, for instance on display size, audio quality and network capacity for watching streaming content. Additionally, queries can be added and edited at runtime. The ordered result of a search for appropriate factories using the factory finder is displayed in a list below. Therefore, context services run on factory devices with location sensors and provide context information to a context manager being queried by the factory finder. For migrating to one of these targets the user has to select the respective factory, choose the component to be moved and press the migrate button (results in invoking `move()` at the *AWSM service*; see Section 3.3.2).

In addition to manually triggered migration, the media player supports automatic migration as well. Therefore, context monitoring is used to get notified about the context profile being violated in the player's current context. This is caused by changed context, such as less network capacity and different user location. By overriding the *AWSM service* method `contextChanged()` the player is able to react to a context violation. Then, it autonomously migrates to another appropriate location. With such a mechanism, behaviour can be implemented, in which the mobile player automatically follows its user, such as described in Section 2.2.2. Therefore, the context profile specifies that the target needs to be located in the user surroundings (described with SPARQL).

A proof-of-concept prototype shows that even time-critical applications benefit from the AWSM approach in conjunction with the context service. In average, migration of the media player between two standard notebooks (Intel Core2 Duo 2 GHz, 1 GB RAM) being connected via 54Mbit WLAN takes only between one and two seconds. This seems to be a reasonable delay. The part of the media stream, which is presented at the original location during the migration process, is replayed at the target location when the player is completely moved to the new location. This is due to the fact that the current player state is transferred during migration. Yet, it allows the user refocusing the presentation.

4.3 Entity Discovery with the Session Initiation Protocol

For many mobile and UbiComp applications, it is essential to discover entities, such as users, devices and services with given characteristics. For instance, in the context of the report application introduced in Section 2.2.3, the rescue coordination centre initially has to discover users with computing devices that are located in the geographical surroundings of the scene.

If the AWSM infrastructure in conjunction with the context service introduced in Section 4.2 was deployed on all these devices, discovering users with particular computing devices in the scene surroundings would not be an issue. Yet, in most cases, this assumption would probably not apply. Thus, this thesis proposes an alternative solution that is implemented on top of standard network infrastructure for next generation networks [ITU04] as proposed by the *IP Multimedia Subsystem* (IMS) specification [3GP09]. IMS has already achieved acceptance among mobile phone[7] service providers and is built on top of the *Session Initiation Protocol* (SIP) [RSC+02], a generic protocol for session management that is a broadly accepted standard for multimedia

---

[7]This thesis advocates that mobile phones have already achieved being ubiquitous. Thus, they can be assumed available in many mobile and UbiComp scenarios, such as the spontaneous reporter scenario of Section 2.2.3.

communication and especially Voice over IP (VoIP). With respect to the mobile report application (see Section 2.2.3), SIP can also be used to send a multimedia message with the needed initial code for the reporter (i.e., a basic AWSM infrastructure with the reporter service facet).

The following sections present a novel SIP-compliant extension that provides a mechanism for registering and discovering SIP endpoints with particular user, device and available service characteristics. It requires only small extensions on top of the classical SIP implementations and obviates the additional overhead of implementing separate discovery services. This approach has several advantages. In the case that there are already SIP entities on the devices, there is no need for another infrastructure providing dynamic discovery of entities. SIP users already have to register with the SIP infrastructure; as a side effect, associated entities (i.e., users, devices and services) can also be registered within one SIP registration transaction. Consequently, the overall network infrastructure complexity is reduced. This can improve the general manageability.

Standard SIP infrastructure relies on central entities that are typically located in the Internet (i.e., SIP registrar and proxy servers as part of the SIP provider network). Thus, it cannot be assumed to function properly in many mobile and UbiComp scenarios, in which an area-wide Internet access cannot be guaranteed (e.g., in disaster management scenarios as described in Section 2.2.3). As a part of this thesis, the author developed a novel decentralised P2P architecture for SIP signalling on the basis of JXTA [Gon01]. The approach does not require any central entities for maintaining the SIP traffic, while preserving compatibility with standard SIP endpoints. As a result, it can for instance be used to build up ad-hoc communication networks by means of a spontaneous point-to-point network between available communication devices within a particular geographic area. Additionally, entity discovery capabilities were seamlessly added into this infrastructure to provide dynamic location of required entities in such environments.

The last part of the chapter evaluates the novel P2P SIP concept in comparison to standard SIP within three scenarios: in addition to an already mentioned point-to-point network, which can be found in many mobile and UbiComp scenarios, local and wide area networks are examined. The results show that the novel P2P approach compares well in terms of response time, especially in the possible mobile and UbiComp setting. Yet, as it employs the standard JXTA routing mechanism, it results in more traffic for maintaining the peer-to-peer overlay.

4.3.1 Session Initiation Protocol

The *Session Initiation Protocol* (SIP) was developed by the Internet Engineering Task Force (IETF) [RSC+02]. The protocol is designed for session management and coordination in general.

4 Infrastructure Services for Mobile and Ubiquitous Computing Environments

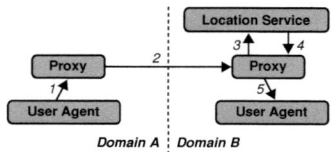

Figure 4.19: Message flow for SIP session establishment

Hence, it allows users to establish, modify and terminate sessions. Today, SIP is widely used for session management of multimedia sessions, such as VoIP, video conferences or Video on Demand (VoD).

SIP is a text-based protocol, which is built upon standard Internet protocols, i.e., the *Internet Protocol* (IP), the *Transmission Control Protocol* (TCP) and the *User Datagram Protocol* (UDP). The client-server model is used as communication paradigm: a request from the client is answered by a response from the server. SIP specifies the behaviour of several network entities: *user agent* (UA), *registrar*, *location service* and *proxy server*.

Figure 4.19 shows the message flow and affected entities for establishing a session. For initiating a session between two terminals, an **INVITE** message is sent. A UA is a logical SIP entity that is responsible for establishing, modifying and terminating sessions. Therefore, it is able to send and to receive appropriate SIP messages. Messages contain a unique SIP URI, which identifies the target UA. They are sent to an initially configured SIP proxy server. SIP proxy servers are responsible for forwarding messages to the target UA. If the target SIP URI is located in a remote domain, the message is forwarded to a proxy server that is responsible for the specific domain (see Figure 4.19, message 2). The address of a responsible proxy is obtained by retrieving an SRV (i.e., service) record from the Domain Name System (DNS) [RS02]. If the receiver is located in the domain of the proxy server, the location service is queried for the actual communication contact address, to which the request is forwarded (message 3–5). The location service stores registration information about available UAs of a specific domain. Therefore, UAs initially have to register their contact data with a **SIP REGISTER** message. This message is sent to a preconfigured registrar, which is able to store the information into the location service.

Figure 4.20 shows a standard SIP call setup between two UAs (i.e., Alice and Bob). As already mentioned before, an **INVITE** request is sent to establish a session. Bob's UA answers with a 180 Ringing response. This denotes that the UA notifies Bob about an incoming session request. When Bob accepts this session request, the UA sends a 200 OK response. Finally, the session is considered established and media data can be transferred after Bob's UA receives an ACK

4.3 Entity Discovery with the Session Initiation Protocol

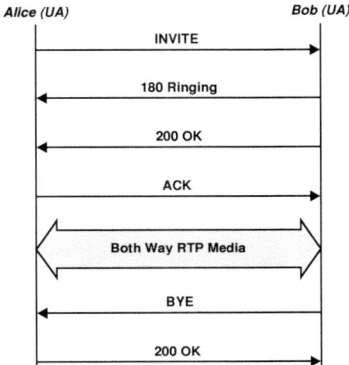

Figure 4.20: Standard SIP call setup and termination between Alice and Bob

request (i.e., session acknowledgement) from Alice. For terminating the session either of them sends a BYE request that has to be answered by a 200 OK response.

By now, the SIP protocol has reached a mature state, which results in a number of stable open source implementations, such as the JAIN SIP protocol stack [NIS09].

4.3.2 SIP Extension to support Entity Discovery

Recent SIP entities rely on using particular entity discovery mechanisms, such as the Service Location Protocol (SLP) for service location [GPVD99]. Yet, an integration of entity discovery into SIP has several advantages, especially if used within an infrastructure that is already based on SIP. There, the standard registration procedure for SIP devices and for associated entities is the same. Combining the registration of both, basic SIP location information and entity descriptions, allows an efficient registration with only one processing step for both registration types. If a separate entity discovery infrastructure was used, the UA would have to register entities after having registered its SIP identity at the registrar. Moreover, using SIP as the only protocol for session management *and* entity location leads to less code at the side of the UAs. There is no need for the implementation of a special entity discovery technique. Yet, a few extra functions on top of a standard SIP implementation for entity registration (i.e., creating the appropriate body messages; see following section) as well as entity discovery have to be added.

4 Infrastructure Services for Mobile and Ubiquitous Computing Environments

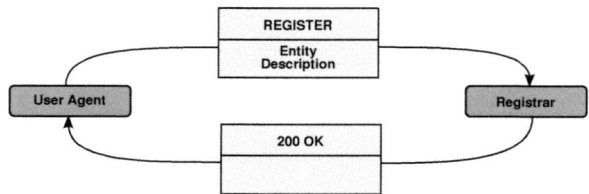

Figure 4.21: Entity registration using SIP REGISTER request

Thus, especially for small/embedded devices in mobile and UbiComp settings, this SIP-only solution is an advantage, as memory and computing power can be saved.

It is also possible to integrate legacy entity discovery servers by using registrars acting as proxy servers. For instance, SIP service registration requests could be transformed to standard SLP requests and then sent to an already available SLP server.

4.3.2.1 Registering Services

For being available to other UAs, UAs initially have to register their identity at the SIP registrar (see Section 4.3.1). It is reasonable to register available entities in a similar way. This thesis proposes a mechanism, in which entity descriptions are sent in addition and together with the basic SIP location information (i.e., current endpoint address) in the SIP REGISTER message. Thus, the registrar acts as a node that collects entity descriptions for later search requests. The information about available entities (i.e., associated with the UA) is attached to the SIP request in the message body (see Figure 4.21).

SIP messages can carry bodies with arbitrary content. Similar to HTTP, SIP body contents are specified by MIME types [Lev98]. For instance, for the establishment of multimedia sessions, the body may contain a message in the format described as Session Description Protocol (SDP) [HJ98]. Yet, bodies can also be used to carry messages of any entity discovery protocol, such as SLP for service location.

Figure 4.22 shows an example of registering a printer service using an SLP description. The registrar extracts this information and stores it in the location service. If the registrar does not support the entity description format, a '415 Unsupported Media Type' error response is returned. In this case, the UA has to repeat the registration request without the attached message body to ensure standard SIP registration. The UA is able to register its associated

4.3 Entity Discovery with the Session Initiation Protocol

```
1   REGISTER sips:registrar.uulm.de SIP/2.0
2   Via: SIP/2.0/TLS client.uulm.de:5061;
3        branch=z9hG4bKnashds7
4   Max-Forwards: 50
5   From: Bob <sips:bob@uulm.de>;
6        tag=a73kszlfl
7   To: Bob <sips:bob@uulm.de>
8   Call-ID: 1j9FpLxk3uxtm8tn@uulm.de
9   CSeq: 1 REGISTER
10  Contact: <sips:bob@client.uulm.de>
11  Content-Type: text/directory;profile="x-slp"
12  Content-Length: 116
13
14  URL: service:lpr://www.uulm.de/598/xyz
15  Attributes: (SCOPE = STUDENTS),
16              (PAPERCOLOR = YELLOW),
17              (PAPERSIZE = A4)
```

Figure 4.22: REGISTER-request containing SLP service description of a printer service

entities with an alternative format or an alternative infrastructure. If the entity description is successfully stored in the location service, a standard '200 OK' response is returned.

4.3.2.2 Searching for Services

This section describes the approach for entity discovery using SIP. Ahead of searching for entities, a UA has to get acquainted with the entity discovery infrastructure. There are different possibilities for the UA to get informed about the available entity discovery service (i.e., possibly offered by the registrar server).

A very basic solution is the static configuration in the client implementation or in a configuration file. Yet, due to the fact that user interactions are required if the infrastructure changes, such solutions are inefficient and error-prone in dynamic mobile and UbiComp environments.

Brunner et al. [BSN05] describe the possibility to configure a UA using Dynamic Host Configuration Protocol (DHCP) extensions [Sch02, SV03]. Yet, this is a very limited solution because it requires DHCP (though, not all devices use DHCP). Additionally, the DHCP server has to be modified for returning the entity discovery configuration data in the responses.

4 Infrastructure Services for Mobile and Ubiquitous Computing Environments

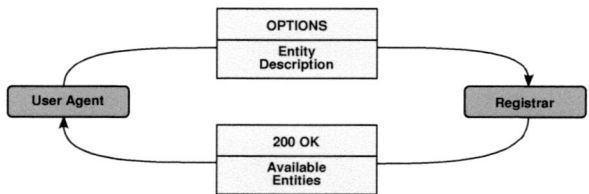

Figure 4.23: Entity discovery using SIP OPTIONS request

A practical solution, especially for UAs on small/mobile devices, is to take advantage of the SIP REGISTER request. This is always the initial step of a UA for attaching to a SIP-enabled network infrastructure. The UA registers at the registrar server with the standard REGISTER request and the response contains information about the entity discovery infrastructure. The REGISTER response contains a Contact header with a SIP or a SIPS URI with a parameter containing *discovery=true* and the supported entity description formats (e.g., *Contact: <sip:user@abc.com;discovery=true;format=slp;>*). A UA capable of the entity discovery mechanism is able to use this information for later discovery processing.

A concrete entity discovery request is initiated by a standard SIP OPTIONS message (see Figure 4.23). In general, OPTIONS is used to determine the capabilities of a UA [RSC$^+$02]. Like other SIP messages, OPTIONS allows attaching arbitrary data that represent the criteria the entities have to satisfy (Figure 4.24 shows an exemplary query describing a printer service for students). First, the discovery server (e.g., the registrar) parses the attached message body. If the server is not able to understand the content a '415 Unsupported Media Type' error response is returned that includes the supported entity description formats in the Contact header. If the server succeeds in parsing the data, it queries the location service for compatible entities. These entities are returned in the message body of a '200 OK' response (if no entities are found, an empty message body is returned).

Another approach keeps entity discovery transparent for the UA. This can be implicitly realised by a smart SIP proxy server. An application of smart proxies based on SIP was already proposed for managing multimedia session configuration [GLK04, GLKM04]. A standard SIP proxy server is not able to use information that is attached to a SIP message. Yet, it is possible to use this information in the proxy server to initiate a search for needed entities, such as users with mobile devices that are located in a given geographical area (see Section 2.2.3). For this purpose, the UA initiates the session such as in the standard case by sending an INVITE request with an appropriate query as message body to the next known proxy server. This proxy server locates

4.3 Entity Discovery with the Session Initiation Protocol

```
1   OPTIONS sip:registrar@uulm.de SIP/2.0
2   Via: SIP/2.0/UDP client.uulm.de;
3         branch=z9hG4bKhjhs8ass877
4   Max−Forwards: 50
5   To: <sip:registrar@uulm.de>
6   From: Alice <sip:alice@uulm.de>;tag=1928301774
7   Call−ID: a84b4c76e66710
8   CSeq: 63104 OPTIONS
9   Contact: <sip:alice@client.uulm.de>
10  Accept: text/directory; profile ="x−slp"
11  Content−Type: text/directory;profile="x−slp"
12  Content−Length: 27
13
14  lpr//(&(SCOPE = STUDENTS))/
```

Figure 4.24: OPTIONS-request containing SLP query

the required devices and automatically involves these entities in the session establishment. The affected UAs cannot distinguish between a standard call-setup and this case [GLSH+06].

4.3.2.3 Updating and Removing Services

For keeping the entity information up-to-date, entity changes must lead to an update of their registration entries at the location service. This can be done as follows:

- A basic approach requires monitoring available entities with respect to the local machine. Whenever a change of the entities is recognised, the UA sends a REGISTER message to the registrar to update the list of available entities. Yet, this naive approach generates a lot of overhead with respect to resources.

- An improved solution is the use of the periodic REGISTER request, with which UAs refresh their registration periodically in order to keep their SIP address 'online' [RSC+02]. This results from the fact that each entry in the location service has a particular expiration time. These successive registrations can also be used to update the state of available entities. The UA checks local entities and sends an up-to-date list of entities as an attachment of the REGISTER request.

Removing entities integrates in SIP as well. For removing a UA and its associated entities a standard deregistration request has to be sent to the registrar. This is done by sending a

REGISTER message containing an expire-value of '0'. In this case, the registrar removes the entry with the information about available entities from the location service. Removing only particular entities is realised by sending a standard REGISTER message that contains only those entities that should remain available in the message body.

4.3.2.4 Basic Security Considerations

It is very important to provide a secure infrastructure for entity discovery. Otherwise UAs relying on the infrastructure could get connectivity problems if the infrastructure becomes unavailable or misbehaves. This is especially the case if the smart SIP proxy approach is implemented due to the fact that UAs are not even able to recognise the difference to standard SIP proxies (see Section 4.3.2.2).

A severe issue is to ensure that only authorised UAs are able to register, update and remove associated entities. Otherwise, malicious UAs are also able to register and replace entities. A UA, which uses these entities, is not able to recognise such possibly malicious entities. Protection can be achieved with standard SIP technologies, such as digest authentication and S/MIME certification [RSC$^+$02]. Other solutions to this security issue can be developed on the basis of lower level (i.e., below SIP) security mechanisms at network access and attachment (e.g., using SIM cards [ETS94] to ensure the authenticity of mobile devices).

Moreover, certificates can also be used with respect to particular entities. Then, UAs are able to decide if they would like to rely on uncertified entities as well.

4.3.3 Decentralised SIP with Extension to support Entity Discovery

Using the proposed traditional SIP infrastructure results in high administrative efforts and potential single points of failure within the network (i.e., proxy and registrar servers). Such requirements do not fit typical mobile and UbiComp scenarios that are characterised by a spontaneous network infrastructure (see Chapter 2.3). With respect to VoIP, Skype [Sky09] started the trend to use P2P techniques to overcome the typical issues of server-based approaches. Yet, in contrast to SIP, Skype uses proprietary protocols for session management lacking interoperability. This inspired efforts to integrate P2P mechanisms into the standard SIP protocol as well.

The key contribution of this section is the presentation of a novel P2P SIP architecture on the basis of JXTA [Gon01]. JXTA allows the integration of arbitrary application layer P2P protocols. This is necessary for supporting different network topologies. For instance, nodes in structured (distributed-hash-table–based) P2P systems are characterised by generating higher maintenance traffic [ESZK04]. Thus, configurability of the P2P routing mechanism can save resources, especially on mobile devices. Unlike recent efforts, such as the approach of *Bryan et al.* [BLJ07] and *Singh et al.* [SS05], the novel architecture is designed on the basis of available standards and open architectures only. The proposed system is standard-SIP–compliant and integrates entity discovery as proposed in Section 4.3.2. The performance results of the prototype show that it is a serious alternative to standard SIP in terms of response time, especially in a typical mobile and UbiComp point-to-point network setting. Yet, maintenance traffic is quite high, which currently restricts the use of the prototype implemented with the default JXTA routing mechanism within mobile networks that are accounted by data volume for reasons of expense.

4.3.3.1 Related Work

Applying P2P techniques to SIP is a popular area of research [BL07]. There is already a lot of work on concepts, terminology, infrastructure, requirements and remaining issues (e.g., the allocation and protection of SIP names) [WBMS07]. Basically, there are two possible approaches to integrate P2P mechanisms into SIP. Either P2P is integrated into the SIP protocol or UAs and proxies rely on a separate P2P service.

Bryan et al. developed a P2P SIP extension called *dSIP*, which uses P2P mechanisms [BLJ07]. The idea is to maintain a P2P overlay on the basis of extended SIP messages serving as a distributed registrar server for resource location. The protocol extension allows publishing and querying contact information, which is required for routing SIP messages without the need of any central server entities. Therefore, additional SIP headers are introduced but no new SIP methods (i.e., message types) are needed. dSIP is designed to support various P2P protocols. In order to guarantee minimal compatibility between potential participants at least Chord has to be supported [ZB07, SMK$^+$03]. dSIP peers (i.e., terminals that are compatible to dSIP) have to provide server-like as well as infrastructure-maintaining functionality, i.e., they have to act like registrar and proxy servers at the same time. In contrast to the work of this thesis. dSIP demands an extended SIP protocol. The approach of this thesis builds on standard SIP and the standardised and open platform JXTA that allows the seamless integration of arbitrary routing mechanisms.

The P2P SIP IETF working group currently follows a different approach. They design *RELOAD*, a lightweight resource location and discovery service [JLR$^+$09a]. It is particularly designed to support P2P SIP. For instance, it ensures unique SIP URIs. Yet, it can be used by other applications as well. If RELOAD is used for P2P SIP, the participating entities use the overlay as a separate storage and lookup service for SIP URIs [JLR+09b]. Thus, for session management, standard SIP can be used. Yet, in contrast to the approach of this thesis, P2P mechanisms are not transparently integrated into SIP. This requires changes to the implementation code of available SIP entities.

With *SIPPEER* Singh and Schulzrinne developed a P2P SIP adaptor, which allows participating into a P2P network without changes to the UA by implementing a P2P SIP proxy [SS05, SS06]. *SIPPEER* should run on the same host as the UA and has to be configured as outbound SIP proxy. Then, all messages of the UA are automatically sent through *SIPPEER*, which provides an extended location service on basis of the *OpenDHT* [RGK+05] infrastructure for registration and discovery (OpenDHT uses the *Bamboo* [RGRK03] P2P implementation as underlying infrastructure). Yet, the approach of this thesis provides a more generic architecture for the integration of P2P technology into SIP by building on standard SIP and JXTA, in which arbitrary routing mechanism can be integrated. This is especially important for devices in mobile and UbiComp settings.

In addition to the state-of-the-art, this thesis integrates P2P-based entity location. Especially in mobile and UbiComp scenarios, where entity location is essential [BSSW03], decentralised techniques can solve typical issues of server-based approaches, such as scalability and high administrative efforts.

4.3.3.2 Design

This section introduces a JXTA-based SIP location service (JXTA-LOC), which can be used by standard SIP entities. This leads to SIP entities that externally behave according to standard SIP but internally use the JXTA-LOC (see Figure 4.25(b), messages 2–3). SIP proxies relying on the JXTA-LOC are able to discover the target UA in the JXTA network and to directly forward messages without the need for further proxies (messages 1 and 4). This results in a reduced session establishment time (in comparison to standard SIP in Figure 4.25(a)). Therefore, registrars also use the JXTA-LOC to store information about UAs in the JXTA network while maintaining standard SIP compliance. The proxy and the registrar should be located locally with respect to the UA for an improved network usage. Yet, a direct integration of the JXTA-LOC into the UA is possible as well. This results in direct communication without the need for proxies but requires code changes at the UA.

4.3 Entity Discovery with the Session Initiation Protocol

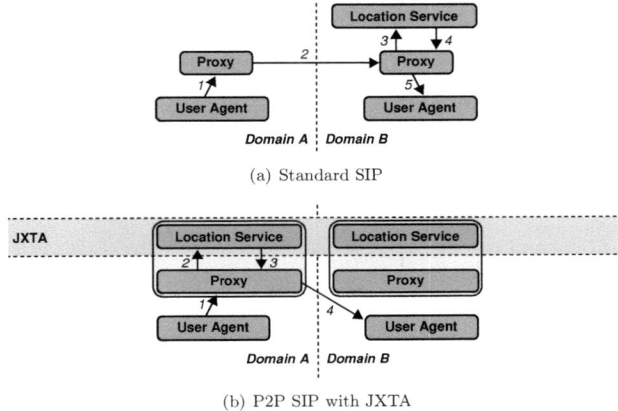

(a) Standard SIP

(b) P2P SIP with JXTA

Figure 4.25: Message flow for SIP session establishment

Additionally, entity discovery was integrated into the concept according to Section 4.3.2. This allows UAs registering associated entities in the JXTA network and searching for them. For instance, UAs are able to search for services when connecting to a new access network, such as a multimedia message service. Alternatively, a UA could also initiate a search for users with mobile devices that are located in a given geographical area, such as required in the report application of Section 2.2.3.

The novel P2P SIP approach on the basis of JXTA allows coexistence with the standard SIP infrastructure. Proxies being responsible for a specific JXTA domain are also able to act as gateways between the different network topologies. This is comparable to traditional telephone network gateways.

4.3.3.3 Implementation with Advertisements

For the implementation of the JXTA-LOC the concept of SIP domains was transferred to JXTA peer groups. Therefore, UAs register their contact information in a specific peer group, which represents the corresponding SIP domain (actually, the peer group name is the SIP domain name with prefix 'sip:').

4 Infrastructure Services for Mobile and Ubiquitous Computing Environments

```
 1  <!DOCTYPE jxta:SIPAdvertisement>
 2  <jxta:SIPAdvertisement xmlns:jxta="...">
 3    <Id>urn:jxta:uuid-0146...5DD301</Id>
 4    <Key>sip:bob@uni-ulm.de</Key>
 5    <Type>jxta:SIPAdvertisement</Type>
 6    <Contacts>
 7      <Contact>sip:bob@134.60.77.162:5060</Contact>
 8    </Contacts>
 9    <Contents>
10      <Content type="text/directory;profile=x-slp">
11        URL: service:lpr://www.uni-ulm.de:598/xyz
12        Attributes: (SCOPE = STUDENTS),
13                    (PAPERCOLOR = YELLOW),
14                    (PAPERSIZE = A4)
15      </Content>
16    </Contents>
17  </jxta:SIPAdvertisement>
```

Figure 4.26: Extended advertisement with printer service information

UA contact information as well as information about associated entities are stored and discovered in the JXTA network by an extended advertisement that contains all needed information (see Figure 4.26). A **Key** represents the publicly addressable SIP-URI, **Contacts** contains the current endpoint addresses of the UA and **Contents** includes the description of associated entities (here, a printer service described using SLP).

SIP registrations are published with associated entity information as advertisements with a given time after which they expire. This time directly maps to a SIP registration **expires** header [RSC[+]02].

Whenever JXTA-LOC–based SIP proxies receive a SIP message, they first extract the target SIP-URI from the SIP request. Then, they search for the advertisement with the corresponding **Key**-field. If they successfully discover an appropriate advertisement, they forward the message on the basis of the **Contacts**-field. Discovered advertisements are stored in a local cache for future use.

Entity discovery is implemented with the SIP OPTIONS message as proposed in Section 4.3.2.2. Particular requests are embedded as SIP attachment and queried by the proxy server on the basis of the **Contents**-field if the format is supported (again, there has to be a type-specific handler, which is able to interpret the contents). Alternatively, the SIP INVITE message allows integrating entity discovery with call-setup (see Section 4.3.2.2). For instance, this allows call-setup within a given area for calling everybody at a specific location for emergency reasons, such as needed in the reporter application (see Section 2.2.3).

4.3.4 Performance Evaluation

This section presents a performance evaluation of the JXTA-based P2P SIP prototype implementation. The needed entities (i.e. UAs and proxy servers) were implemented with JAIN SIP 1.2 [NIS09] and JXTA 2.4. Additionally, a standard SIP location service was implemented on the basis of a standard Java `Hashtable` as data store.

4.3.4.1 Testbed Description

The concept was evaluated with *ns-2* [FV09], an open-source discrete event simulator supporting networks with various topologies. For gaining realistic results the emulation feature of ns-2 was used that imitates a given network configuration to the application. This allows considering timing behaviour, which is important for evaluating P2P applications. The emulated nodes run on top of User-Mode Linux [Dik06], a virtual machine running Linux. This approach allows running the application to evaluate in a standard Linux environment, in which network traffic is intercepted and injected into the ns-2 network simulator, without any modifications to the application. For each simulated network node, a User-Mode Linux process is started. The emulation was performed on an AMD Athlon XP 2500 with 512 MB RAM.

4.3.4.2 Scenario Description

The novel P2P SIP approach was evaluated with three scenarios.

- *local area network* (LAN): a small switched network with 15 machines, which are connected with 100Mbit/s data rate with 2ms latency.

- *point-to-point network* (PTP): 30 randomly meshed machines with an average of 0.5Mbit/s data rate with 10ms latency.

- *wide area network* (WAN): four LANs connected by a router; 100Mbit/s connection within the LANs with 10ms latency; 5Mbit/s connection between LANs with 50ms latency.

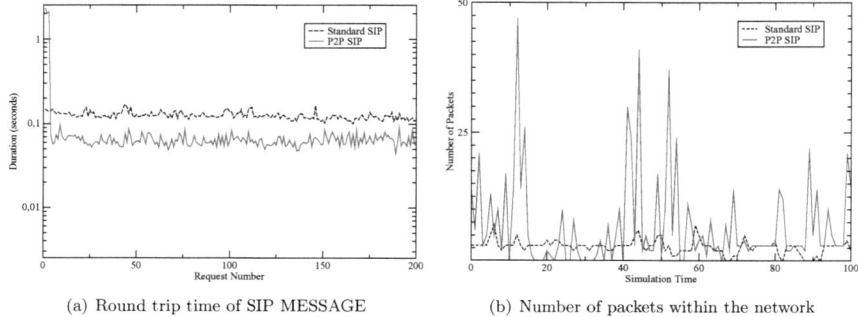

(a) Round trip time of SIP MESSAGE (b) Number of packets within the network

Figure 4.27: Local area network

In all scenarios, one sender was deployed, which rotationally sends 319 byte SIP MESSAGE requests to three identical receivers on predefined nodes. In the P2P SIP scenarios, a JXTA-based proxy/registrar server was deployed on the receiver and sender node, whereas in standard SIP scenarios proxy servers were placed on different nodes within the networks. In the LAN and the PTP scenario, the sender and receiver applications were deployed on random but distinct nodes, in the WAN scenario on random nodes within different LANs.

4.3.4.3 Results

This section shows the results of evaluating the prototype within the aforementioned scenarios. Firstly, Figure 4.27 shows the evaluation of the round trip time of sequential SIP MESSAGE requests and the number of SIP and JXTA packets within the network with respect to the simulation time in the LAN scenario. It is obvious that the first requests in the P2P SIP scenario take much longer than in the standard SIP case. This is due to the JXTA discovery process: when the SIP proxy receives the MESSAGE request, it queries the JXTA network for the actual contact address of the target UA. In the standard SIP scenario, this is performed by DNS, which is apparently faster because of its centralised nature. After the third request (i.e., three receivers), the round-trip time of P2P SIP is lower than in the standard SIP setting because the target address is already cached (see Section 4.3.3.3). This saves at least one hop because in P2P SIP there is no more need for the proxy server within the target UA's domain

4.3 Entity Discovery with the Session Initiation Protocol

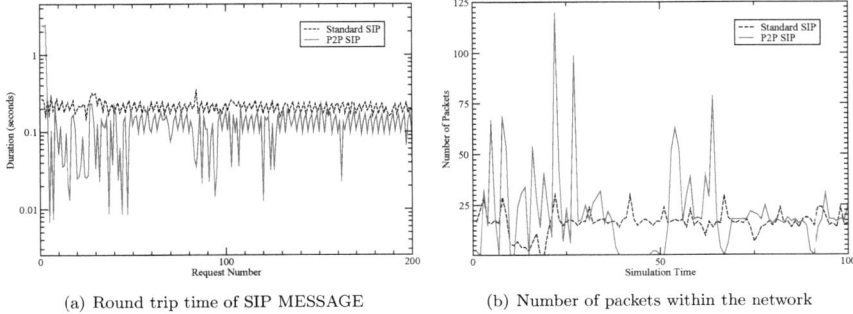

(a) Round trip time of SIP MESSAGE   (b) Number of packets within the network

Figure 4.28: Point-to-point network

(see Figure 4.25). The number of packets in P2P SIP is higher because of JXTA discovery, which is based on local broadcast, and the JXTA maintenance traffic.

Secondly, Figure 4.28 evaluates the round trip time of sequential SIP MESSAGE requests and the number of packets within the network according to the simulation time in the PTP scenario. Such as in the previous LAN scenario, the round-trip times of the first P2P SIP requests are higher than of standard SIP, and lower from the fourth request on. This is again due to the JXTA discovery process and caching mechanism. The variance in round-trip time, especially for P2P SIP, is higher compared to the LAN scenario because of the randomly meshed topology and therefore not predefined routing of SIP messages within the PTP network. The number of packets in P2P SIP is again higher compared to standard SIP. In comparison with the LAN scenario, the number of packets in P2P SIP is higher because of the randomly meshed nature of the PTP scenario.

Thirdly, Figure 4.29 evaluates the round trip time of sequential SIP MESSAGE requests and the number of packets within the network according to the simulation time in the WAN scenario. Again, the round-trip time of the first P2P SIP messages is higher than with standard SIP, but is lower from the fourth request on because of JXTA discovery and caching mechanisms. The variance is higher compared to the LAN scenario but lower compared to the PTP scenario because of the predefined routing paths with one particular router connecting the four LANs. The number of packets in P2P SIP is again much higher in comparison with standard SIP because of JXTA discovery and maintenance traffic. Yet, compared to PTP, the number of packets is

4 Infrastructure Services for Mobile and Ubiquitous Computing Environments

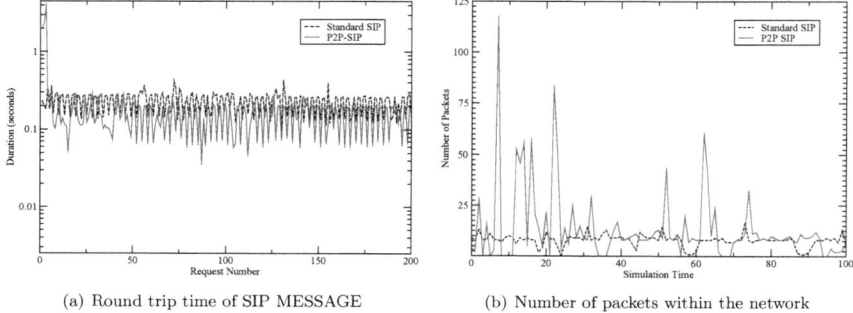

(a) Round trip time of SIP MESSAGE (b) Number of packets within the network

Figure 4.29: Wide area network

lower because of the JXTA rendezvous peer concept, which reduces inter-LAN communication by introducing a super peer structure.

In all scenarios, the first requests take considerably longer. This could be improved by periodically searching for advertisements in the domain. This results in more addresses being cached. Yet, such an approach reduces the response time but increases the overall traffic. Another alternative to decrease the initial lookup time would be the use of an improved customised JXTA routing mechanism.

P2P SIP reduces administrative tasks as it does not require the management of central servers. Thus, it is predestined for already self-organising PTP networks, such as in (wireless) mesh networks that are present in many mobile and UbiComp settings. The author additionally measured the scalability of P2P SIP in comparison to standard SIP in the PTP scenario. Figure 4.30 shows that the number of overall packets increases with the number of actively participating entities because of the JXTA discovery and maintenance traffic. This results in a relatively high data volume, which leads to high costs in networks that are accounted by data volume (e.g., mobile phone networks). Yet, due to the fact that the P2P SIP approach is built on top of standard JXTA, it is possible to replace the standard routing protocol with a particular protocol for mobile networks without having to change the prototype.

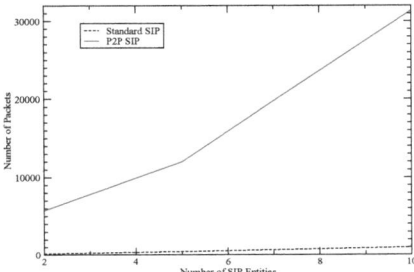

Figure 4.30: Number of total packets during simulation according to participating SIP entities in point-to-point network

4.4 Soap*ME*: A Lightweight Java ME Web Service Container

With UbiComp becoming reality there is a great potential of computing power in the surroundings. This can be provided by mobile devices such as mobile phones and PDAs building spontaneous networks. A possible approach is resource provisioning in terms of services following the paradigm of the service-oriented architecture [Bar03]. For service provisioning, Web services are an accepted standard. As already mentioned, this thesis advocates that these can also be used in mobile and UbiComp scenarios (see Section 3.3.2). Moreover, Web services especially support the heterogeneous nature of mobile and UbiComp environments by building on XML technology to implement interoperable communication. Yet, most available Web service containers do not consider the demands of resource-limited devices.

The *Java Micro Edition* (Java ME) provides a Java environment for small mobile devices, such as PDAs and mobile phones. It requires only minimal resources and provides two configurations, i.e. the *Connected Device Configuration* (CDC) and the *Connected Limited Device Configuration* (CLDC). CDC is intended for powerful devices, whereas CLDC is running on resource-limited devices as well. Therefore, CLDC uses a Kilobyte VM (KVM)—a minimal virtual machine (VM)—instead of a standard JVM. Among several runtime restrictions, CLDC has no support for reflection and custom dynamic class loading. Thus, each class has to be deployed within the same archive as the running application (i.e., MIDlet).

This section presents Soap*ME*, a novel SOAP-based Web service container for Java ME. Soap*ME* is very lightweight. For supporting as many devices as possible Soap*ME* is based on CLDC because CLDC-compatible applications are also running in a CDC environment [Sun06a]. Having broad acceptance in the Web service community, SOAP [W3C07b] is used for Web service invocations. Unlike related work, Soap*ME* provides dynamic deployment of SOAP-based Web services at runtime. The Soap*ME* prototype provides several extension points, for instance for invocation interception and changing the transport protocol. It shows reasonable performance on a standard mobile phone and is compliant to the standard SOAP *test collection* specification. Thus, Soap*ME* perfectly suits mobile and UbiComp settings.

Up to now, there is no comparable Web service container for Java ME CLDC. There exist several Web service containers for standard Java, such as Apache Axis [Apa06] but there is only one very rudimentary Java ME CLDC Web service container (i.e., JME SOAP Server [Sou06a]). In contrast to Soap*ME*, JME SOAP Server does not provide any extension points and does not support dynamic deployment at all.

The following section gives a broad overview on related work.

4.4.1 Related Work

There is a lot of work on client-side access to Web services. Amongst others, Apache Axis provides such an implementation for standard Java environments [Apa06]. *KSoap* [Sou06b] provides even a client-side SOAP framework for Java ME CLDC environments. Furthermore, there is a Java ME Web services specification by Sun providing an optional package for client-side SOAP Web service access (JSR 172 [EY04]). However, the focus of Soap*ME* is only Web service provisioning. Thus, client-side access is merely needed for testing purposes.

There are Web service containers for several platforms. Most of these containers restrict themselves to a standard JVM and are characterised by high resource demands in terms of CPU, physical memory and disk space. There are Web service containers for Java ME as well but these are either incomplete or do not support CLDC environments. Both variants, standard Java as well as Java ME Web service containers, are described in the following.

4.4.1.1 Standard Java Web Service Containers

Apache Axis [Apa06] is a SOAP-based Web service container. For providing its full functionality, it requires a Java Servlet container such as Apache Tomcat [Apa09b] as runtime environment. Axis comprises a three-layer architecture. A transport layer provides an abstraction from the transport channel, a SOAP layer from SOAP-specific tasks, and a service layer from service-specific tasks. Each layer can contain chains to perform specific behaviour via interception. Axis supports SOAP versions 1.1 and 1.2 and Web service descriptions using WSDL [W3C07e]. WSDL documents are created on demand by accessing a specific Uniform Resource Location (URL). Axis is a very rich Web service container focusing on a standard Java environment. The resulting hardware and software requirements disqualify Axis from being used on resource-restricted devices, such as in mobile and UbiComp scenarios.

There are other Web service containers as well, such as *Metro* [Sun09c]. Metro can be used as a standalone Web service container or embedded into a standard Java Servlet container. Metro shows equal platform restrictions as Axis by supporting only standard Java environments. Thus, it cannot be used in a Java ME CLDC environment with support for resource-limited devices.

4.4.1.2 Java ME Web Service Containers

JME SOAP Server [Sou06a] is a Web service container for Java ME CLDC. Similar to Apache Axis, it splits the invocation process into transport-, SOAP- and service-specific components. For simulating the missing reflection of CLDC, custom wrappers are used for a generic invocation method. Unlike Soap*ME*, these wrappers have to be implemented manually. Additionally, there is a tight coupling between services and the container, which lacks dynamic deployment. It is impossible to extend the container for dynamic deployment without a complete refactoring.

Srirama et al. presented an approach for mobile Web service provisioning [SJP06]. For a prototype implementation *PersonalJava* [Sun09b] is used. Yet, it does neither support Java ME CLDC nor dynamic Web service deployment. This disqualifies its use for mobile and UbiComp scenarios.

DPWS4j [SOA08] is a Web service stack, which is compliant to the Device Profile for Web Services specification [Mic06]. However, it demands for powerful devices running Java ME CDC.

4.4.1.3 Summary

Overall, there is no reasonable Web service container for Java ME CLDC. Yet, there are alternatives for standard Java environments and there are even some basic approaches for small devices. Nevertheless, these approaches for small devices do not support dynamic deployment.

4.4.2 SoapME Requirements

The author identified several requirements concerning the Soap*ME* Web service container for Java ME. The following basic requirements should be supported:

- *Support for Java ME CLDC* to support as many resource-limited devices as possible.
- *SOAP as communication protocol* because SOAP is the common communication protocol for Web services. Due to the fact that many clients support SOAP version 1.1 but only few support version 1.2, Soap*ME* should support both in order to be future-proof.
- *Dynamic Web service deployment at runtime* because it provides a powerful instrument in dynamic mobile and UbiComp scenarios avoiding a restart of the Web service container.
- *Manageability* in order to increase the acceptance. This includes several stakeholders: service consumer, provider, developer and system developer. For each stakeholder the handling of installation, removal and configuration should be manageable. Each kind of stakeholder has a particular view of the Web service container which has to be considered.
- *Extensibility* for covering future features and special requirements. This includes extensions such as further communication protocols, transport protocols and interceptors.

In addition to the basic requirements, there are platform requirements as well. As a software requirement, Soap*ME* demands for the support of server sockets providing the underlying communication. Server sockets are only supported in Java ME MIDP 2.0. [JSR06], which leads to specific hardware requirements (e.g., minimum display size of 96x54px, minimum main memory of 384kB and basic network capabilities).

4.4.3 SoapME

This section first introduces the architecture of Soap*ME* with details on the architectural components and their local communication. Then, it presents the concept for dynamic Web service deployment at runtime.

4.4.3.1 Architecture

The architecture of Soap*ME* is split-up into a central *generic Web service proxy* and several *custom Web service providers* (see Figure 4.31). Both components contain parts of the Web service framework. Soap*ME* provides the Web service proxy, which delegates received SOAP

4.4 SoapME: A Lightweight Java ME Web Service Container

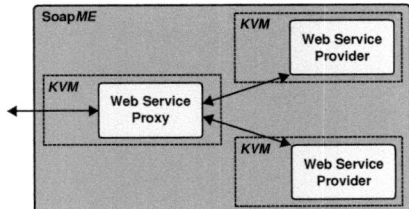

Figure 4.31: Soap*ME* architecture

requests to the corresponding Web service provider. The custom Web service provider has to be implemented by the developer. It executes the service call and returns an appropriate response to the Web service proxy. The Web service proxy creates and returns the corresponding SOAP response.

Such a proxy delegation pattern allows dynamic deployment of Web services. Therefore, the Web service proxy enables installing Web service providers at runtime. Due to the fact that Java ME CLDC does not allow dynamic loading of code at runtime, the Web service proxy as well as Web service providers are implemented as MIDlets and thus run within their respective own KVM to support the dynamic deployment of Web services at runtime (see Section 4.4.3.2). However, Java ME does not provide standard inter-MIDlet communication[8]. Thus, Soap*ME* uses local sockets (see below).

Web Service Proxy The Web service proxy performs all mapping and delegation tasks between the client and the Web service endpoint. Therefore, a request is initially processed by the SOAP processing chain, which consists of three containers (i.e., transport, SOAP and service container; see Figure 4.32). The transport container abstracts from the particular network channel and transport protocol in use. Then, requests are delegated to the SOAP container, which performs SOAP syntax checks, abstracts from the SOAP message and checks if the service exists. The service check is important to save essential runtime resources. Otherwise, resources would be reserved and CPU runtime consumed even if the corresponding service was not available. Finally, the service container invokes the service using local socket communication with the Web service provider. For this purpose, a mapping from the service name to the local service port is used (the service name is extracted by the local transport channel). In case of an error in the request processing chain, a SOAP fault is immediately returned omitting the remaining containers.

---
[8]This is a feature that will be part of MIDP 3.0 [Mot09], which has not yet been approved.

4 Infrastructure Services for Mobile and Ubiquitous Computing Environments

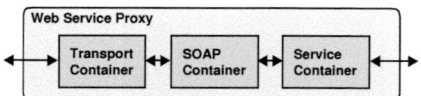

Figure 4.32: Web service proxy SOAP processing chain

With respect to the basic SOAP process, the Web service proxy is part of a Model-View-Controller (MVC) architecture [Ree79]. All view tasks are enclosed in a GUI-providing part of the Web service proxy. Controller tasks are performed in the containers of the SOAP processing chain. The model (i.e., the data) is stored in the particular Web service providers or in record stores (i.e., a basic kind of database for Java ME applications).

Web Service Provider Unlike the Web service proxy, the Web service provider invokes the actual Web service endpoint. Therefore, it maps SOAP-specific data structures of the service request to Java data structures and invokes the locally registered Web service. In general, Web services have a specific service style [W3C07e]. Soap*ME* has built-in support for document- and RPC-based services. Other style variants are possible and can be integrated with reasonable effort (by an extension of the `Service` interface, see Section 4.4.4). Depending on the service style, a service is called via a `DocumentStyleWrapper` or an `RPCStyleWrapper`. These objects manage necessary transformations and call the service in a style-specific way. For performing generic service invocations, the service-style layer is abstracted using a `WebServiceStyleWrapper`. The wrapper object receives a simple SOAP Message with several `ComplexType` and `SimpleType` objects. For this purpose, mappings between SOAP and Java data types are specified in an encoding style. Considering SOAP there is a default SOAP encoding style [W3C07c], which is supported by Soap*ME*. As a basic extension mechanism, further encoding styles, which are identified by a specific URI, can be registered at an encoding style registry.

Generic functionality for Web service providers is encapsulated into the abstract class `WebServiceMIDlet`, which can be extended by custom Web service provider implementations. The abstract class includes the creation and management of the endpoint for interaction with the Web service proxy. Thus, service developers do not have to implement the required communication behaviour (see below).

Services are registered with their respective service-style at a common `ServiceRegistry` using a unique service-name. Interceptors can be specified at the same time as well. An `Interceptor` object is able to manipulate input and output service parameters. This allows extending the architecture according to individual needs. Among the service parameters are `SimpleType`, `ComplexType` and `ServiceObject` objects. A `SimpleType` represents a basic data type, such as a String, and a `ComplexType` is used for unknown complex structures, such as a SOAP struct. A `ServiceObject` extends `ComplexType` by providing support for self-designed SOAP structs with a particular Java mapping for deserialisation and serialisation. Each `ServiceObject` has to be registered at a `ServiceObjectRegistry`.

With respect to the missing reflection support of CLDC, services have to offer a static interface for generic invocation support. Therefore Soap*ME* introduces two generic delegation methods; one for document and one for RPC style invocations. In a document style invocation a complex element represents the whole document, while in a RPC style invocation the method name and parameters can be used by the called method to delegate the invocations to the particular method implementations (see Section 4.4.4).

Local Communication The local communication between the Web service proxy and the Web service provider is implemented with bidirectional sockets (see Figure 4.31).

An incoming message is parsed at the Web service proxy to recognise faults as soon as possible. To avoid another costly XML parsing step at the service provider and to reduce the communication overhead, the local communication does not use XML. Instead, Soap*ME* introduces a basic communication format, which is powerful enough to transfer the relevant information.

An Extended Backus-Naur Form (EBNF)-like notation of the basic Soap*ME* communication format is shown in Figure 4.33. It specifies three types of objects: *simple type*, *complex type* and *fault*. A simple type represents a simple request message element with text as content. A complex type is a request message element with sub elements (simple types and complex types). The complex type uses the encoding style of the SOAP request as this implies no need for transformation at the Web service proxy and allows service-specific encoding styles. The third object type is the fault object. It abstracts from the message exchange for SOAP faults. In contrast to the other object types, it is only sent from the Web service provider to the Web service proxy. In case of fault detection at the Web service proxy, the requesting client is notified without informing the corresponding Web service provider.

Incoming request messages are first split-up into a header and a body part. Then, for both message parts, single elements are encoded as simple and complex types and then send to the Web service provider via the socket. The Web service provider invokes the endpoint and returns an encoded message that may also contain simple types, complex types and faults. Then, the Web service proxy creates and returns an appropriate response to the client.

4 Infrastructure Services for Mobile and Ubiquitous Computing Environments

```
 1  Type ::= SimpleType | ComplexType | Fault
 2
 3  SimpleType ::= 's' sname id snamespace attribute sdata
 4  sname ::= value
 5  snamespace ::= value
 6  sdata ::= reference | normal
 7  reference ::= 'r' value
 8  normal ::= 'n' stype value
 9  stype ::= value
10
11  ComplexType ::= 'c' cname id [cnamespace] [encoding] [ctype] [prefix] [attribute] cdata
12  cname ::= 'n' value;
13  cnamespace ::= 'ns' value
14  encoding ::= 'e' value;
15  ctype ::= 't' value;
16  prefix ::= 'p' value;
17  cdata ::= 'd' <int> Type;
18
19  Fault ::= 'f' code reason description
20  code ::= value;
21  reason ::= value;
22  description ::= value;
23
24  id ::= value
25  attribute ::= 'a' value;
26  value ::= <int> <chars>
```

Figure 4.33: Grammar of local communication format

4.4.3.2 Dynamic Deployment

Dynamic deployment of Web services is a crucial part of Soap*ME*. It allows installing and removing of Web services at runtime. Hence, Soap*ME* provides a deployment service, i.e., a standard Web service with an interface for installation and removing of arbitrary Web service providers at runtime. Therefore, remote deployment services are used: deployment services allow listing of as well as searching for all downloadable Web service providers (i.e., services managed by the deployment service that can be downloaded and deployed).

The deployment service is implemented as a standard Web service with RPC style. Its functionality as well as the installable Web service provider packages are delivered by an `HttpServer`, which implements a basic socket-based channel and an extended Bluetooth channel. Thus, it is also possible to discover and install a service with standard Bluetooth mechanisms. This is especially useful in mobile and UbiComp scenarios with spontaneously connecting devices.

In the Soap*ME* prototype, the deployment service answers a search request with a SOAP struct containing `DeploymentInformation`. This struct comprises information, such as the service name, service information and a Bluetooth address. The Bluetooth address is embedded to accelerate the service discovery process (otherwise, any Bluetooth device in the surrounding area could answer the query, which would require filter mechanisms). Internally, `DeploymentInformation` is registered at a `DeploymentInformationRegistry`, which is used by the deployment service to manage available services.

As already described in Section 4.4.3.1, Web service providers run within their own KVM as standard MIDlet. For dynamic deployment these have to be started on demand after the necessary code has been loaded. Yet, in general, Java ME CLDC does not allow starting MIDlets out of another MIDlet. There are several Java ME extensions and libraries, which can be used to start applications. Yet, these are restricted to specific vendor platforms and devices. A possible approach to overcome this issue is using the standard push registry [Ort03], which allows initial registration of MIDlets to a specific port. Then, in case of an incoming connection at this port, the MIDlet is automatically started if it is not already running. Due to the fact that the push registry is a standard component of Java ME MIDP 2.0 the author favours this approach to maintain standard compliance.

Depending on the capabilities of the respective device, a specific installation process is chosen. If the device supports the push registry and allows file system access, a custom configuration file containing the particular push registry port to use is built on the device. In case of push registry support without support for file system access, the custom installation file containing the respective push registry port is built on server side and then loaded to the device. If there is no push registry support, the installation file is installed via the basic Java ME over-the-air (OTA) provisioning mechanisms [JSR06].

Dynamic deployment of Web services leads to security issues, which are common to dynamic deployment of applications in general (see Section 4.1.5). To provide at least some kind of basic security, Soap*ME* makes use of standard Java ME security mechanisms, such as signing of code.

```
1  public interface Service {
2    public Object callMethod(String method,Vector params,Vector inContext,Vector outContext)
         throws ProcedureNotFoundException;
3    public Object call(Object o,Vector inContext,Vector outContext) throws
         ProcedureNotFoundException;
4  }
```

Figure 4.34: `Service` interface

```
1  public abstract class ServiceObject extends Type {
2    public abstract Vector getValues();
3    public abstract void set(String name, Object value);
4    public abstract Object get(String name);
5  }
```

Figure 4.35: Abstract `ServiceObject` class

4.4.4 Service Development

For creating a custom Web service provider a MIDlet has to be implemented. Therefore, the abstract class `WebServiceMIDlet` provides generic code for socket and record store management. This frees the developer from implementing low-level logic. The actual Web service endpoint has to implement a specific `Service` interface (see Figure 4.34). The `call()` method is invoked in case of document-style calls, whereas the `callMethod()` method is invoked in case of RPC-style calls. Due to the missing reflection in Java ME CLDC, both methods provide means for a single invocation entry point, which is used for dispatching the invocations to the actual implementation methods. The dispatching logic has to be implemented by the developer; however, there is a basic code generation tool that was created as part of this thesis, which creates the corresponding class of a given interface with the dispatching logic. The `inContext` and `outContext` parameters implement the Web service context (e.g., client identification or a session cookie) and are directly mapped to SOAP headers.

In case of user-defined Java Beans as parameters, the corresponding class extending `ServiceObject` has to be registered with a qualified name at the `ServiceObjectRegistry` (implements serialisation and deserialisation; see Section 4.4.3.1). Without this registration, such a parameter would be handled as a `ComplexType`. Figure 4.35 shows the abstract `ServiceObject` class. The abstract methods overcome the missing reflection support of Java ME CLDC. They have to be implemented by the Java Bean developer in order to dispatch invocations to the right getter and setter methods. In addition to complex data types, Soap*ME* supports vectors and

```
1  public interface Interceptor {
2    public void doIntercept(ComplexType msg, byte version);
3  }
```

Figure 4.36: `Interceptor` interface

```
1   public class HelloWorldWebService implements Service{
2     public Object call(Object o, Vector inContext, Vector outContext) throws
            ProcedureNotFoundException {
3       if (o != null && o instanceof SimpleType) {
4         // invoked method is sayHello?
5         if (((SimpleType)o).getName().equals("sayHello")) {
6           // ok, send response!
7           return new SimpleType("echoHelloWorld","Hello "+((SimpleType)o).getValue());
8         }
9         ...
10      }
11      // something bad happened...
12      return null;
13    }
14    ...
15  }
```

Figure 4.37: Hello World service implementation

primitive data types. Vectors are mapped to SOAP arrays and primitive data types to their XML Schema equivalent.

The Web service endpoint (i.e., implementing the `Service` interface) has to be registered at the `ServiceRegistry`. This implies the specification of the service name, invocation style and possible interceptors. The latter can be called before or after a service invocation and have to implement the `Interceptor` interface (see Figure 4.36). An interceptor has only one method, which expects the whole abstracted Web service message as `ComplexType`. This allows changing the whole message in a very flexible manner.

Figure 4.37 shows an exemplary *Hello World* Web service implementation for document-style invocations. The communication between the Web service proxy and the provider is transparent for the Web service endpoint. A Web service provider only has to ensure the handling of all data types.

4 Infrastructure Services for Mobile and Ubiquitous Computing Environments

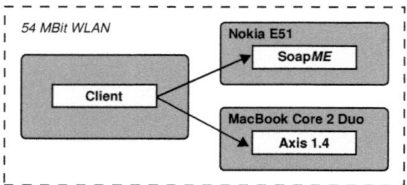

Figure 4.38: Evaluation setup

4.4.5 Evaluation

This section shows a brief evaluation of the SoapME prototype. First, it describes tests regarding standard SOAP compliance and then it presents a performance evaluation with respect to service invocation in comparison to Apache Axis.

4.4.5.1 Compliance

For measuring the compliance of SoapME the SOAP conformance test collection [W3C07d] was used. SoapME achieves positive results regarding SOAP body processing with handling of SOAP structures, arrays, references and SOAP faults.

Header processing was not implemented as part of the Web service proxy as it is not required for most applications. Thus, this functionality is not part of the SoapME basic infrastructure to keep it as small as possible. For achieving compliance to the *SOAP conformance test collection* regarding header processing, this functionality has to be manually implemented within the respective Web service provider using the `inContext` and `outContext` parameters (see Section 4.4.4).

4.4.5.2 Performance

SoapME is implemented with strong consideration of runtime and performance issues. For instance, due to the restricted resources of mobile devices running Java ME CLDC, SoapME performs manual garbage collection when large memory blocks can be freed (e.g., after a service invocation).

Figure 4.38 shows the setup to measure the performance of SoapME. The Web service proxy and the Web service provider run on a Nokia E51 mobile phone with a 369MHz CPU and

4.4 SoapME: A Lightweight Java ME Web Service Container

Service	Platform	Invocation Style	Response Time (ms)		
			Average	Minimum	Maximum
Hello World	SoapME	sequential	554	521	571
		parallel	1703	631	2764
	Axis 1.4	sequential	15	10	20
		parallel	20	10	30
Java Bean	SoapME	sequential	637	611	671
		parallel	2311	1642	3084
	Axis 1.4	sequential	36	10	321
		parallel	41	10	360

Figure 4.39: Evaluation of service invocation duration

96MB RAM. For comparison, an Apache Axis version 1.4 Web service container runs on a MacBook Core 2 Duo with a 2GHz CPU and 2GB RAM. In both scenarios, a standard Java client connects via a 54Mbit WLAN connection to the particular Web service container using a standard socket connection. Then, the time duration of sending a SOAP request until receiving the corresponding response was measured. Therefore, the client sends 100 requests and measures the average duration in case of sequential as well as parallel requests (100 parallel threads for the requests in the Java client). This was measured for two scenarios: a basic Hello World service and complex Java Bean interaction (`DeploymentInformation` as parameter, see Section 4.4.3.2), which was implemented for SoapME and Apache Axis.

Figure 4.39 shows the evaluation results. An important fact to note is that a simple ping request in the scenario takes 200ms to the Nokia E51 and only 2ms to the MacBook. This results from the fact, that the performance of the socket implementation on Java ME is poor; even local communication between the Web service proxy and the actual Web service provider takes about 120ms in average. If socket communication via WLAN was left out, a Hello World request with SoapME takes 354ms in average, while it takes 13 ms with Apache Axis. The Java Bean interaction provides similar results but the first Axis invocation takes 321ms due to Axis-internal initialisation. In general, we think that SoapME provides reasonable performance with respect to the resource limitations of its evaluation platform. As soon as that there is an improved socket implementation, this can drastically improve overall performance of SoapME because of the local socket communication. Moreover, until now there is no comparable Web service container running on top of Java ME CLDC, which makes SoapME unique.

4.5 Summary

This chapter introduced four services to support application developers implementing sophisticated applications for typical mobile and UbiComp settings:

1. A dynamic code management service
2. A generic context service
3. An entity discovery service on the basis of SIP
4. Soap*ME*, a lightweight Java ME Web service container

First, the chapter presented a generic and decentralised approach to dynamically discover, select, load and integrate platform-specific code on demand. This is a highly essential service in dynamic mobile and UbiComp scenarios as implementation code cannot be assumed to be available (i.e., pre-installed) on all possible devices in advance. In the proposed approach, specific implementation code is automatically selected on the basis of functional and in particular non-functional properties. Section 4.1.2 provided an elaborate discussion of the necessity of considering non-functional properties in such a system. According to the common P2P idea, every peer within the infrastructure is able to load code and also to provide this code on demand. The prototype implementation extends and improves the mechanisms for dynamic code loading of JXTA. Yet, the proposed generic concept can be applied to any P2P infrastructure that at least supports keyword search. Additionally, Section 4.1.4 showed a transparent integration of DCM into OSGi. In contrast to related approaches, the OSGi prototype allows centralised and decentralised sharing and discovery of bundles and services at runtime. Moreover, resources are automatically selected on the basis of functional and particularly non-functional properties. Finally, Section 4.1.4.5 presented a performance evaluation of the prototype in comparison with the OBR and Section 4.1.4.6 showed a seamless integration of the prototype into AWSM.

Secondly, Section 4.2 sketched the design of a generic context service with a generic context model. Providing a notion of context is essential in mobile and UbiComp settings to support run-time decisions, such as if an application should be fundamentally adapted. For the implementation only standards were used, such as OWL for describing and SPARQL for querying and monitoring context. The approach builds up a highly modular and thus extensible architecture, which allows adding context components and their sensors at runtime. The context service provides a standard Web service interface. This eases the integration with mobile and UbiComp infrastructures, such as AWSM, by providing high interoperability due to standard-compliant interaction. With the seamless integration of the context service, AWSM becomes a powerful mobile and UbiComp platform.

Thirdly, Section 4.3 presented a novel approach of integrating entity location into SIP. Such a mechanism is essential in many mobile and UbiComp scenarios, in which specific entities have initially to be discovered (e.g., mobile report application introduced in Section 2.2.3). It provides a lightweight alternative if the generic context service is not available. The solution integrates well with the SIP protocol by keeping standard compliance while being able to flexibly transport any entity description format. Thus, the approach can be used in any SIP-capable networks, such as proposed by IMS, which is currently used to implement next generation mobile phone networks. The combination of entity discovery with session management has the benefit that instead of using separate protocols, only one SIP stack is needed for both, session management and entity discovery. Thus, SIP-only management reduces resource usage on embedded and mobile devices as many of these devices already provide a SIP stack to consume VoIP services. Additionally, Section 4.3.3 presented a novel P2P architecture for SIP signalling on the basis of the generic and open P2P platform JXTA. Thus, it obviates the need for central proxy servers, which results in a self-organising P2P network without the need for central servers. Such a topology especially fits spontaneous mobile and UbiComp scenarios, such as introduced in Section 2.2. Yet, the approach still guarantees compatibility to standard SIP entities and seamlessly integrates entity discovery. Section 4.3.4 showed an evaluation of the concept within a broad range of scenarios: in addition to a typical mobile and UbiComp PTP network setting, a WAN and a LAN scenario. Overall, the results show that the P2P SIP approach with JXTA provides good response time but results in more traffic for maintaining the P2P overlay in comparison to standard SIP.

Finally, Section 4.4 presented Soap*ME*, a highly flexible and lean Web service container for Java ME CLDC. It was designed and implemented with a strong focus on the support of resource-limited devices in order to provide a generic communication platform for mobile and UbiComp scenarios. Soap*ME* has a code size of only about 200kB and supports dynamic deployment of Web services at runtime. Therefore, it requires support for multiple running KVMs on the device (e.g., supported by Nokia E51). Soap*ME* offers several extension points, for instance request/response interception and integration of arbitrary transport protocols (e.g., binary XML instead of standard SOAP). The evaluation proves SOAP 1.2 conformance and reasonable performance on a Nokia E51 mobile phone. To the best of the author's knowledge, Soap*ME* is the first Web service container for Java ME CLDC providing dynamic deployment and reasonable performance.

5
Development Support

This thesis proposes *AWSM services* to implement applications in mobile and UbiComp scenarios (see Section 3.5). *AWSM services* provide means to fundamentally adapt an application in terms of its location (i.e., weak service migration), available state, provided functionality and implementation in use. At the same time, *AWSM services* maintain a unique service identity that allows addressing the Web service independent of its current fundamental adaptation state (required to foster the collaboration between different applications). Although *AWSM services* provide great flexibility for fundamentally adaptive applications, developers have to manually implement the actual adaptation logic.

This section presents a model-driven approach to ease the development of fundamentally adaptive applications on the basis of *AWSM services*. Therefore, the concept of a *self-adaptive mobile process* (SAMProc) is introduced in Section 5.1, which provides a novel abstraction for fundamentally adaptive applications. The basic idea is to describe the application as a SAMProc and to use this information to automatically generate the fundamental *AWSM service* adaptation logic with a tool.

As a novel description language, Section 5.2 presents the *Self-adaptive Mobile Process Execution Language* (SAMPEL), an XML application to describe a SAMProc. Due to the fact that the

Business Process Execution Language (BPEL) already provides means for orchestration of *standard* Web services, SAMPEL is implemented as a BPEL extension, which additionally supports describing *AWSM service* behaviour regarding fundamental adaptation. Section 5.2.2 shows a tool, which automatically generates the fundamental adaptation logic of the corresponding *AWSM service*. Thus, developers have to implement the pure application logic only.

Moreover, Section 5.3 introduces an Eclipse plug-in that allows describing fundamentally adaptive applications with a graphical notation. Modelling with the Eclipse plug-in leads to an automatic generation of an appropriate SAMPEL description. Thus, in the overall process, the SAMProc approach allows generating the fundamental adaptation logic of an adaptive application with only a few clicks.

In comparison to related work, such as proposed by *Ishikawa et al.* [ITYH06] and *DEMAC* [KZL06], the SAMProc approach is more lightweight at runtime because node-tailored code is generated, which is not interpreted but executed at runtime. Yet, more details on related work can be found in Section 5.4.

5.1 Building Adaptive Applications with Self-adaptive Mobile Processes

This section sketches the novel approach of specifying applications on the basis of a *self-adaptive mobile process* (SAMProc). It is defined as follows:

> *A self-adaptive mobile process provides a high-level abstraction for fundamentally adaptive applications. Internally, it can be seen as an ordered execution of activities. It is able to fundamentally adapt itself in terms of state, functionality and implementation to the current context and to migrate either for locally executing services at the target or for accessing a particular context, while maintaining its unique identity.*

The basic idea is that application developers should be able to model a fundamentally adaptive application with its interactions and deployment aspects as a SAMProc following the idea of the model-driven architecture (MDA) [OMG03]. MDA aims at separating pure functionality from the implementation technology. Therefore, it allows specifying high-level models, which are transformed into concrete implementations by an automatic code generation process.

Figure 5.1 shows the overall transformation and code generation process in the context of the mobile report application introduced in Section 2.2.3. In the first step, the application developer

5.1 Building Adaptive Applications with Self-adaptive Mobile Processes

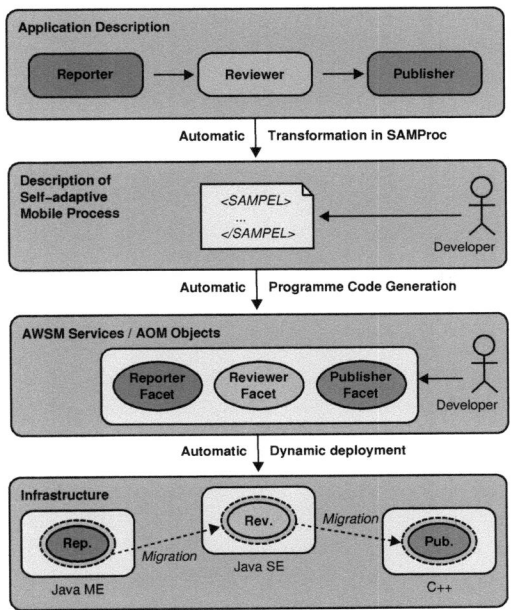

Figure 5.1: MDA-like development of a SAMProc

models the required application functionality as well as interactions and deployment aspects as a SAMProc (see Section 5.3). Then, this model is automatically transformed into a SAMProc description represented by the novel description language SAMPEL (see Section 5.2). At this step, the application developer is able to manually refine the SAMProc description. In the next step, a tool automatically generates the *AWSM service*[1] application code from the SAMProc description (see Section 5.2.2). The presented tool is able to automatically create code skeletons for all required implementations (i.e., Web service facets) of a SAMPEL process description. These code skeletons have already built-in support for fundamental application adaptation. Thus, the developer only has to implement the pure application logic. Finally, the application code is distributed using the DCM service as described in Section 4.1.

---

[1]Yet, such a tool could generate appropriate *AOM object* code as well (see Section 3.3.1).

5 Development Support

The following sections present the model-driven approach to ease the implementation of fundamentally adaptive applications with *AWSM services*.

5.2 Self-Adaptive Mobile Process Execution Language

This section introduces the *Self-adaptive Mobile Process Execution Language* (SAMPEL) as a novel XML application to describe SAMProcs. SAMPEL is an extension of BPEL [OAS07], which is an XML application commonly used for describing business processes that are realised by Web services. Such a business process consists of the involved Web service interfaces, the interaction between them and a process state. Thus, BPEL is commonly characterised as a means for orchestration of Web services to build a business process. Like Web services, BPEL uses WSDL to describe the involved Web service interfaces. Moreover, a BPEL process itself is offered as a Web service. It is interpreted by BPEL engines, such as *ActiveBPEL* [Act09].

The way to describe processes with BPEL is suitable for describing SAMProcs as well. Yet, BPEL does not meet all requirements for SAMProcs. First, BPEL was particularly designed for business processes with focus on orchestration of Web services whereas SAMProcs rely on advanced concepts such as application facets and active process state. BPEL lacks support for these concepts. Additionally, BPEL processes are designed to be executed at a static location, whereas SAMProcs provide concepts for fundamental adaptation with support for migration. Hence, BPEL does not provide the indispensable support for distribution aspects of SAMProcs. For instance, before migrating, a SAMProc has to select an appropriate location. Therefore, it needs context information about possible targets, such as available resources, being matched with its own context requirements. BPEL has to be extended for describing such required context. Furthermore, current devices being used in mobile and UbiComp environments are highly resource-limited. Thus, it is in general not feasible to run a BPEL engine on these devices due to its high resource usage. Unlike BPEL, the SAMPEL process is not interpreted by a particular SAMPEL engine but used for node-tailored code generation. Additionally, SAMPEL supports fundamental adaptation of a SAMProc. There, the process is able to fundamentally adapt itself according to the current execution platform.

The following section presents the SAMPEL description language in detail. Particular importance is attached to the extensions of BPEL. Then, Section 5.2.2 introduces a tool for the automatic generation of *AWSM service* code on the basis of SAMPEL.

```
1  <process ... >
2     ...
3     ACTIVITIES+
4  </process>
```

Figure 5.2: Basic BPEL process description

5.2.1 Description Language

Like BPEL, a SAMPEL description is always paired with at least one WSDL description, which declares the SAMProc interfaces (i.e., the interfaces of the application facets being implemented by the SAMProc).

5.2.1.1 Processes and Instances

A crucial difference between BPEL and SAMPEL is the conceptual view on a process. A BPEL process is an instance within a BPEL engine and always has similar behaviour (e.g., starting with accepting a purchase order, then communicating with the involved Web services and eventually informing the purchaser about the shipping date). Unlike this, a SAMPEL process (i.e., a SAMProc) is characterised by a highly dynamic behaviour since it can get fundamentally adapted by even changing the execution location at runtime, where it exists as an instance and handles user interactions (e.g., the mobile report application; see Section 2.2.3). Additionally, SAMProcs provide means to change the process state at runtime. Due to the inherent dynamics, a SAMPEL process is more functional oriented as opposed to a BPEL process (i.e., SAMPEL focuses on process functions instead of offering predefined process behaviour, such as in the purchase order example). This difference is reflected in the BPEL description by the placement of activities.

Figure 5.2 shows the process definition of a BPEL process with its activities. Activities specify the process behaviour, such as invoking an application and assigning a value to a variable. A BPEL process has activities in the main scope, whereas a SAMPEL process has not. Due to the functional oriented design, the activities of a SAMPEL process are basically determined by the activities within method definitions (i.e., **eventHandler**; see below). Figure 5.3 shows the basic layout of a SAMPEL description. The **process** element contains all remaining parts of a SAMProc, which are explained in more detail in the following.

5 Development Support

```
1   <process ... >
2     <partnerLinks>+
3       ...
4     </partnerLinks>
5     <variables>?
6       ...
7     </variables>
8     <correlationSets>
9       ...
10    </correlationSets>
11    <eventHandlers>
12      ...
13    </eventHandlers>
14  </process>
```

Figure 5.3: Basic SAMPEL process description

```
1   <scope>
2     <partnerLinks>?
3       ...
4     </partnerLinks>
5     <variables>?
6       ...
7     </variables>
8
9     ACTIVITIES+
10  </scope>
```

Figure 5.4: Basic SAMPEL scope description

5.2.1.2 Scopes

A scope is a container for activities. As such, it is a structuring element that forms the control sequence of other elements. There are two kinds of scopes, the main scope of a process and its sub-scopes. The main scope is implicitly defined by the **process** element and contains global variables, correlation sets and methods as shown in Figure 5.3. It must contain at least one method definition. Otherwise, the process has no activities. Sub-scopes (i.e., local scopes) can be defined by the **scope** element. As shown in Figure 5.4, sub-scopes must contain activities to be executed as part of the scope and can contain elements that are used by the activities within the scope or its sub-scopes, such as local variables.

5.2 Self-Adaptive Mobile Process Execution Language

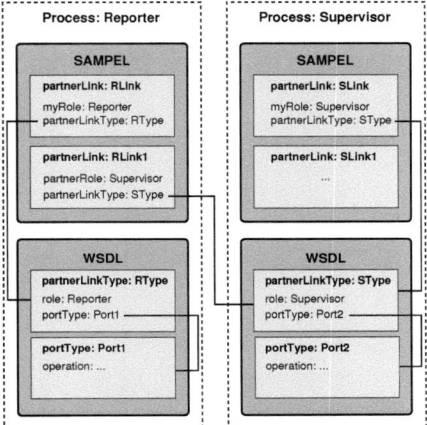

Figure 5.5: Partner links

5.2.1.3 PartnerLinks

Partner links are a SAMPEL concept inherited from BPEL. They allow declaring the communication endpoints of the SAMPEL process and its partner services. SAMPEL allows declaring partner links in the main scope as well as in sub-scopes. Figure 5.5 shows the concept of partner links illustrated for the mobile report application. There, both processes—the reporter and the supervisor[2]—are represented by their SAMPEL description and WSDL description. Each process describes its communication endpoint by means of a partner link (i.e., RLink for the reporter process and SLink for the supervisor process). Each partner link relates to a partner link type of its WSDL description, which works as a bridge between partner links and a specific WSDL port type (contains the available operations for the communication). The same applies to the endpoints of other services (see Figure 5.5 for the partner link RLink1 which links to the partner link type SType of the supervisor process). These definitions allow referring to communication partners within the process description.

Figure 5.6 outlines the corresponding definition of partner links in a process description and

---
[2]i.e., the mobile report application was extended with a particular supervisor entity that provides information about currently required information. This can highly increase the report quality.

5 Development Support

```
1   <!-- SAMPEL -->
2   <process name="Report" xmlns:rpt="e1.wsdl">
3     <partnerLinks>
4       <partnerLink myRole="Reporter"
5                    name="RLink1"
6                    partnerLinkType="rpt:RType" />
7     </partnerLinks>
8   </process>
9
10  <!-- WSDL -->
11  <definitions targetNamespace="e1.wsdl"
12              xmlns:plnk="http://schemas.xmlsoap.org/ws/2003/05/partner-link/"...>
13    ...
14    <plnk:partnerLinkType name="RType">
15      <plnk:role name="Reporter"
16                 portType="tns:ReportPortType" />
17    </plnk:partnerLinkType>
18  </definitions>
```

Figure 5.6: Partner link example

a WSDL description. The upper part with the `process` element belongs to the SAMPEL description and the lower part with the `definitions` element to the corresponding WSDL description. A partner link must be defined inside a `partnerLinks` container element and is composed of a role (denoted by the `myRole` attribute), a name (denoted by the `name` attribute) and the partner link type (denoted by the `partnerLinkType` attribute). The name of the partner link is referred within the process description to specify a communication endpoint for an activity. The role and partner link type refer to the WSDL description to select the WSDL port type for that communication endpoint. Due to the fact that WSDL does not inherently provide the ability to define partner link types, they are injected into the WSDL description by means of an additional partner link namespace. As shown in Figure 5.6, a partner link type has a name (denoted by the `name` attribute) and must have at least one `role` element inside. A partner link from the process description points to a specific `role` element in the WSDL description by following the role and the name of the partner link type. Eventually, the `role` element refers to a WSDL port type with its `portType` attribute.

5.2 Self-Adaptive Mobile Process Execution Language

```
1  <variables>
2    <variable name="report" type="xsd:string" />
3    <variable name="recID" messageType="rpt:ID"/>
4    ...
5  </variables>
```

Figure 5.7: Variable description example

5.2.1.4 Variables

An important means for storing temporary values or maintaining the process state are variables. SAMPEL allows variable declarations in the main scope and sub-scopes with the **variable** element. The variables in the main scope are global variables and are treated as the implementation-independent process state (i.e., considered for migration; see Section 3.3.2). Variables within sub-scopes are local variables used by activities in the sub-scope and its nested sub-scopes. Figure 5.7 shows an example for two variable declarations with respect to the report application. A variable must be declared within the **variables** container and is composed of a variable name (denoted by the **name** attribute) and a data type for the value. The data type can be declared either using an XML schema type (denoted by the **type** attribute; see Figure 5.7, line 2) or as a reference to a WSDL message type (denoted by the **messageType** attribute; line 3).

5.2.1.5 Correlation Sets

SAMProcs are created at a particular location. Then, they are able to fundamentally adapt by migrating to other locations. Thus, there can be multiple instances of the same SAMProc at the same location. For distinguishing between them, SAMPEL inherits the concept of correlation sets from BPEL to create a unique identifier. It is composed of two parts in the form **process-id.instance-id**. The process identifier identifies the SAMPEL description and the instance identifier identifies an actual process instance of that process description. The instance identifier is derived from one correlation set only. Therefore, it must be defined within the **process** element.

Figure 5.8 shows how to define a correlation set for identifying a mobile report application instance within SAMPEL and WSDL. Correlation sets have to be defined in the process description inside a **correlationSets** element and consist of a name (denoted by the **name** attribute) and properties (denoted by the **properties** attribute). The name of a correlation set is referenced from within the process description, whereas the properties have to be defined in the corresponding WSDL description (i.e., properties must be mapped to message types defined in

5 Development Support

```
1   <!-- SAMPEL -->
2   <process ... >
3     <correlationSets>
4       <correlationSet name="ID"
5         properties="rep:ReporterID rep:ReportNr" />
6       ...
7     </correlationSets>
8     ...
9   </process>
10
11  <!-- WSDL -->
12  <definitions xmlns:vprop="http://docs.oasis-open.org/wsbpel/2.0/varprop" ...>
13    ...
14    <vprop:property name="ReporterID" type="xsd:int" />
15    <vprop:propertyAlias propertyName="ReporterID" messageType="inMsg" part="ID" />
16    ...
17  </definitions>
```

Figure 5.8: Correlation set to identify report instance

the WSDL description[3]). This way, correlation to an instance can be determined from incoming messages. All properties are represented by a **property** element that has a name (denoted by the **name** attribute), is of particular XML schema type (denoted by the **type** attribute) and can be assigned to a WSDL message type by means of a **propertyAlias** element. The property alias refers to a property with its **propertyName** attribute and to a WSDL message type with its **messageType** attribute. If the WSDL message type has more than one part, the **part** attribute addresses the appropriate part of the WSDL message type with its name.

5.2.1.6 Methods

The behaviour of SAMPEL processes is basically described by the activities within their methods, which are specified with the **onEvent** element. Figure 5.9 specifies a **setReport** method as part of the mobile report application. An **onEvent** element requires several mandatory attributes: a reference to a partner link that declares the communication endpoint, the port type of the partner link (needed in case of several available port types), a name for the method (denoted by the **operation** attribute) and a message type that declares the input of the method.

---

[3]The vprop-namespace (http://docs.oasis-open.org/wsbpel/2.0/varprop) inherited from BPEL allows to extend WSDL with the capability to describe properties.

5.2 Self-Adaptive Mobile Process Execution Language

```
1   <eventHandlers>
2    <onEvent partnerLink="ReporterPL"
3            portType="ReporterPT"
4            operation="setReport"
5            messageType="ReportMsg"
6            variable="Message" >
7     <correlations>
8       <correlation set="ReporterCS" />
9     </correlations>
10
11    <requires>
12      <property key="role" value="Reporter" />
13    </requires>
14
15    <scope>
16     ...
17    </scope>
18   </onEvent>
19   ...
20  </eventHandlers>
```

Figure 5.9: SAMPEL: method description for reporter

In addition to these mandatory attributes, there is an optional **variable** attribute that implicitly creates a local variable in the scope of the method and fills that variable with the values submitted at method invocation. Moreover, each method must have a scope for activities and a reference to the correlation set to use (to address the right instance on the basis of the received message).

5.2.1.7 Distribution Aspects

Distribution aspects are specified with the **requires** element, which can be placed as part of an **onEvent** element (see Figure 5.9, line 11–13). It can also be placed before an activity and thereby effect only the following activity. Figure 5.10 shows a basic example where the scope is restricted to the reviewer role (i.e., abstract facet; see Section 3.2.1). A **property** element requires a key (denoted by the **key** attribute) and a value (denoted by the **value** attribute). SAMPEL allows multiple properties inside the **requires** element, which are interpreted as follows. If two properties have different keys, then the values are linked in a logical 'and' manner. They are

5 Development Support

```
1  <requires>
2    <property key="role" value="Reviewer" />
3  </requires>
4  <scope>...</scope>
```

Figure 5.10: SAMPEL example for distribution aspects

```
1  <invoke partnerLink="SupervisorPL" operation="getRequiredInfo" portType="SupervisorPT" >
2    <toParts>
3      <toPart part="ID" fromVariable="varId" />
4    </toParts>
5    <fromParts>
6      <fromPart part="RequiredInfo" toVariable="varRequiredInfo" />
7    </fromParts>
8  </invoke>
```

Figure 5.11: SAMPEL: invocation at supervisor

linked in a logical 'or' manner in case of the same keys. This forms a property set with key/value-pairs that restricts an activity. SAMPEL allows specifying SPARQL queries as well. There, the key of the property element is denoted by 'sparql-query' and the value contains the SPARQL query. In case of a SPARQL query only additional 'role' property elements are allowed. This feature to describe requirements regarding distribution is unique to SAMPEL (i.e., not part of BPEL).

5.2.1.8 Basic Activities

Activities determine the behaviour of a process. Therefore, SAMPEL inherits BPEL activities. There are structuring activities and basic activities, which differ in such that structuring activities form the execution flow of nested structuring or basic activities. For instance, two basic activities can be either executed sequentially or in parallel depending on the surrounding structuring activity. Basic activities actually contribute to a process step and are essential elements, such as a variable copy operation and waiting for an answer.

Communication with other applications is covered by the **invoke** activity (see Figure 5.11 for an invocation at the supervisor within the report application). For invoking an application (e.g., a Web service), a partner link of the desired application has to be specified (denoted by the **partnerLink** attribute). Furthermore, the name of the operation has to be provided and an

```
1  <receive partnerLink="SupervisorPL" operation="getRequiredInfo" portType="SupervisorPT" >
2    <fromParts>?
3      <fromPart part="RequiredInfo" toVariable="varRequiredInfo" />
4    </fromParts>
5  </receive>
```

Figure 5.12: SAMPEL: wait for an invocation at the supervisor

```
1  <reply partnerLink="SupervisorPL" operation="getRequiredInfo" portType="SupervisorPT"
      variable="result" />
```

Figure 5.13: SAMPEL: replying to an invocation at the supervisor

optional port type can be specified. Parameters of the invocation are specified with the **toPart** element.

Waiting for an invocation can be specified with a **receive** activity. Figure 5.12 shows how to define such an activity with an example waiting for an invocation from the mobile report application at the supervisor. This is similar to an **invoke** activity for the partner link, operation and port type. These attributes address a communication endpoint to wait for. The received message can be copied to local variables.

Sending a reply to an invocation is an important activity for communication with other applications. A **reply** element either corresponds to an **onEvent** or a **receive** element (i.e., there has to be a partner link to identify the corresponding element). As shown in Figure 5.13, a variable containing the return value has to be provided. In comparison with standard programming languages, a **reply** activity for an **onEvent** immediately replies to the caller but does not necessarily stop the **onEvent** activity. This allows executing activities even after the **reply**.

Assigning a value to a variable is done by the **assign** activity, which copies a value to a destination variable. Within the **assign** element, multiple **copy** elements are allowed. Each **copy** element performs a copy operation to a previously declared variable. Figure 5.14 shows an example.

Explicitly waiting is possible with the **wait** element. It allows specifying a blocking wait state either for a particular duration or until a given date and time. Duration is specified as a value of the XSD schematype **duration** (see Figure 5.15 for an explicit wait for one minute) while date and time are given as a value of the XSD schematype **dateTime** (e.g., '2009-12-24T12:00+01:00' for Christmas 2009). For instance, this can be used as part of polling sequences.

5 Development Support

```
1  <assign>
2    <copy>
3      <from>
4        <literal>this is the result ...</literal>
5      </from>
6      <to variable="result" />
7    </copy>
8  </assign>
```

Figure 5.14: SAMPEL: assigning a variable

```
1  <wait>
2    <for>PT1M</for>
3  </wait>
```

Figure 5.15: SAMPEL: explicit wait for one minute

Extensible activities allow describing custom SAMPEL activities. Figure 5.16 shows how to define an extensible activity with the **activity** element. There, an activity is defined that supports reporters with spell-checker functionality. There is only one attribute allowed, which denotes the activity name. For instance, in a corresponding *AWSM service* implementation, such an activity is mapped to an abstract method (supported by the code generator; see Section 5.2.2), which has to be implemented by application developers. Thus, developers are able to use advanced programming language features within extensible activities that cannot be specified with pure SAMPEL. In contrast to SAMPEL, this feature is not supported by BPEL.

Explicit middleware support for fundamental adaptation is realised by the **copy** and **adapt** elements. These elements are not supported by BPEL. The **copy** activity creates a copy of the instance and assigns it a new instance identifier. The **adapt** element contains a property set (this is equal to the property set in Section 5.2.1.7). According to the given fundamental adaptation properties, the process is able to fundamentally adapt in terms of location, state, functionality and implementation. Figure 5.17 shows an example that requests a fundamental adaptation of the mobile report application into the reviewer role. For instance, a corresponding *AWSM service* implementation (see Section 5.2.2) is able to pass the property set to the AWSM platform, which automatically handles the required steps to implement the SAMPEL description.

```
1  <activity name="spellCheckReport" />
```

Figure 5.16: SAMPEL: extensible reporter activity

5.2 Self-Adaptive Mobile Process Execution Language

```
1  <adapt>
2    <property key="role" value="Reviewer" />
3  </adapt>
```

Figure 5.17: SAMPEL: fundamental adaptation to reviewer facet

```
1   <if>
2     <condition>string−length($report)&lt;=100</condition>
3     <adapt><property key="Mem" value="1MB"/></adapt>
4     <elseif>
5       <condition>string−length($report)&lt;=1000</condition>
6       <adapt><property key="Mem" value="5MB"/></adapt>
7     </elseif>
8     <else>
9       <adapt><property key="Mem" value="10MB"/></adapt>
10    </else>
11  </if>
```

Figure 5.18: SAMPEL: conditional fundamental adaptation

5.2.1.9 Structuring Activities

Structuring activities form the control sequence for basic activities and can be arbitrarily nested in order to build up complex control sequences. The first sub-scope of a method represents the top-level structuring element for starting a control sequence. It contains basic activities and structuring activities. Any structuring activity can contain further sub-scopes. Basic activities can be executed in sequence by enclosing them with a **sequence** element. Execution in parallel can be performed with the **flow** element, which starts each activity at the same time and ends when the last activity has finished. SAMPEL also offers constructs for conditional execution as known from traditional programming languages. Figure 5.18 outlines the usage of an **if**/**elseif**/**else**-construct for the mobile report application. The condition given within the **condition** element has to be an XPath expression that evaluates to a Boolean value. Further conditional execution constructs are loops described with the **while** and **repeatUntil** elements. Both evaluate an XPath expression to repeat the containing activities. The difference is that the **while** element stops as soon as the condition evaluates to a Boolean **false**, whereas the **repeatUntil** stops if the condition evaluates to a Boolean **true**. For instance, for a corresponding *AWSM service* implementation, sequential and conditional activities can be mapped to corresponding programming language constructs, whereas parallel activities should use threads.

5 Development Support

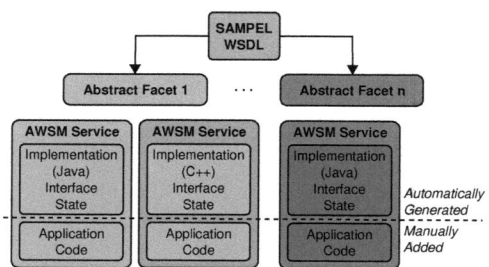

Figure 5.19: SAMPEL code generator

5.2.2 Automatic Code Generation

For implementing the model-driven approach with the SAMProc concept, code skeletons for the respective *AWSM service*[4] implementations have to be automatically generated from the SAMPEL description (see Section 5.1). This section presents a Java code generator for this task. It keeps pure application logic written by application developers separated from generated implementation skeletons by generating abstract classes. This allows developers extending[5] and customising the implementations with the pure application logic.

Figure 5.19 shows the overall code generation process. The code generator uses the SAMPEL description and all referenced WSDL documents to generate code skeletons for the required *AWSM service* facets. In general, code generation for any programming language would be possible. Yet, this work introduces a code generator for Java.

For each generated implementation, an XML file is created that holds meta data about the *AWSM service* facet and its implementation. This allows the AWSM platform to register the implementations and take meta data into account regarding fundamental adaptation decisions.

Finally, the generated *AWSM service* facet skeletons (i.e., abstract classes) contain fundamental adaptation support and programming-language–dependent realisations of the activities specified with SAMPEL. This includes the fundamental adaptation logic. Thus, developers only have to add the pure application logic to implement their application on the basis of an *AWSM service*.

---
[4]The automatic generation of implementation code for *AOM objects* is also possible but not part of this thesis.
[5]Java does not allow multiple inheritance. This is a severe issue if application developers have to extend other classes as well. Yet, application developers can implement the same behaviour with delegation [GHJV95].

5.2 Self-Adaptive Mobile Process Execution Language

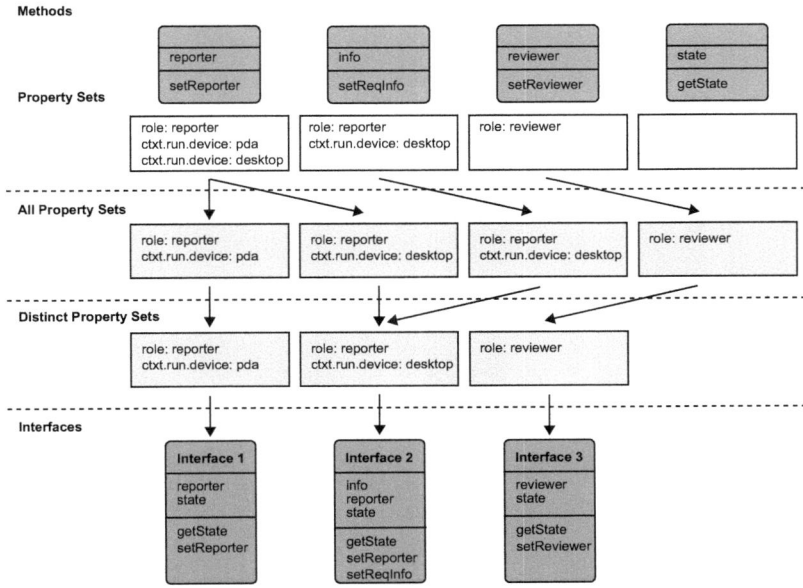

Figure 5.20: SAMPEL code generation: determination of interfaces and respective state

5.2.2.1 Abstract Facets

For each *AWSM service* facet (i.e., abstract facet; see Section 3.2.1), the code generator first determines the interface (i.e., a set of methods) and available state. Figure 5.20 illustrates the process of identifying the set of needed interfaces on the basis of the mobile report application. For this purpose, the code generator analyses the property sets of the method definitions within the SAMPEL description (a method describes its property set with the **requires** element; see Section 5.2.1.7). The distinct sets out of all property sets of the method definitions determine the required abstract facets[6]. Thus, each abstract facet provides a particular set of properties, which

---
[6] If a property set contains properties with the same name (i.e., linked in a logical 'or' manner; see Section 5.2.1.7), these property sets are first expanded: all required property sets are created in such a way that these altogether reflect the original property set but each property set only contains properties with distinct names.

5 Development Support

determine the methods building up the overall interface. For completing a specific abstract facet, the respective active state is determined by identifying the global variables being used within the methods of the corresponding interface (see Figure 5.20).

For each abstract facet, the generation process starts with the main scope and recursively generates the content using the sub-elements, such as methods, sub-scopes and activities.

5.2.2.2 Methods

Explicit SAMPEL methods (i.e., specified with the `onEvent` element) are implemented with conventional programming language methods with the following exception. Due to the fact that SAMPEL methods allow activities even after replying to a request (e.g., with a standard `return` instruction in Java), the instructions of each method are wrapped into a custom Java thread, which continues with activities while the requested method can reply to the invocation. Figure 5.21 illustrates the generic structure of a generated method. Variable exchange with the Java thread is implemented with a global hash table `methodVariables` (see Section 5.2.2.4). The key of a particular variable is the concatenation of the method name, message type and the variable name. The return value is also put into the hash table. For the key, the method name, message type and 'returnValue' are concatenated. Thus, the overall task of the generated method is to copy the required values to the hash table (see Figure 5.21 lines 2–5), start the activity thread (lines 7–9 and 15–23), wait for the return value (line 10) and eventually return with the value from the hash table (line 12).

Implicit SAMPEL methods are defined with the `receive` activity, which waits for an incoming message. In case of a correlating `reply` activity, the method has a return value. Just as with explicit methods, the task of an implicit method is the message exchange as well as the synchronisation with the associated basic activities.

5.2.2.3 Activities

Most basic activities are implemented using their direct programming language counterparts. For instance, extensible activities result in abstract methods that have to be implemented by application developers. These methods have a context parameter that for instance allows accessing local variables. Overall, extensible activities provide a very powerful mechanism to implement custom behaviour with full Java programming language support, such as direct user interaction with a Java GUI.

5.2 Self-Adaptive Mobile Process Execution Language

```
 1  public returnType MethodName (type1 par1, ...) throws Exception{
 2    /* initialize  method variables with arguments */
 3    if (par1 != null)
 4      methodVariables.put ("MethodName.MsgType.par1", par1);
 5    ...
 6
 7    Thread methodNameMsgTypeContext = new Thread(new MethodNameMsgTypeContext());
 8    synchronized (methodNameMsgTypeContext) {
 9      methodNameMsgTypeContext.start();
10      methodNameMsgTypeContext.wait();
11    }
12    return (returnType) methodVariables.get("MethodName.MsgType.returnValue");
13  }
14
15  class MethodNameMsgTypeContext implements Runnable {
16    public void run() {
17      try {
18        /* Activities */
19        ...
20      }
21      catch (Exception e) {...}
22    }
23  }
```

Figure 5.21: SAMPEL: Java code for an explicit method definition

Web service invocations are implemented on the basis of Apache Axis (yet, in case of a prototype for Soap*ME*, kSOAP [Sou06b] could be used as well). Figure 5.22 shows the structure of the generated Java code for a Web service invocation. The service endpoint (line 3) is determined using the partner link attribute of the **invoke** element. As already described in Section 5.2.1.3, the partner link relates to a partner link type element in a referring WSDL document. The WSDL document contains at least one binding with a service endpoint address. The required operation name, parameters and the return type (Figure 5.22, lines 4–6) are part of the **invoke** element as well.

For mapping the fundamental adaptation logic to a particular *AWSM service* implementation, the property set of a fundamental adaptation request is passed through to the AWSM platform, which automatically manages the needed steps as described in Section 3.3.2. Figure 5.23 shows the necessary code.

5 Development Support

```
1  Service service = new Service();
2  Call call = (Call) service.createCall();
3  call.setTargetEndpointAddress (new URL(http://...));
4  call.setOperationName("operation");
5  call.addParameter(..., ParameterMode.IN);
6  call.setReturnType(...);
7  Object result = call.invoke (new Object[] {...});
```

Figure 5.22: SAMPEL: Java code for Web service invocation

```
1  // <adapt>
2  //   <property key="role" value="Reviewer" />
3  //   <property key="sparql-query" value="..." />
4  // </adapt>
5
6  adapt("<requires><property key='role' value='Reviewer' /><property key='sparql-query'
         value='...' /></requires>");
```

Figure 5.23: SAMPEL: Java code for fundamental *AWSM service* adaptation

Structuring activities, such as conditional execution, are mapped to their programming language counterparts. The `flow` element is implemented as a thread to achieve parallel execution.

5.2.2.4 Variables

All variables of the main scope are mapped to member variables that are marked as implementation-independent state with the appropriate annotation (see Section 3.3.2.4).

Due to the `flow` elements and method threads, a high number of threads are in general involved to implement a SAMPEL description. This makes accessing variables that are not part of the main scope difficult. Hence, the generated implementations use a global hash table `methodVariables`[7]. The key is determined by the concatenation of the path of class names (i.e., inner classes and thread classes) and the name of the variable. For reasons of code readability, the global hash table is hidden by generated getter and setter methods for each variable. Figure 5.24 shows an example accessing the variable `var1`.

All getter and setter methods can be overwritten by inner classes. This mechanism ensures the validity of variables according to SAMPEL scopes. Finally, assigning variables with SAMPEL is directly mapped to the respective getter and setter methods.

---
[7]This is also the common approach of current BPEL engines, such as ActiveBPEL [Act09], to execute BPEL.

```
1   class Outer{
2     int var1;
3     public void var1 (int arg){ // Setter
4       ...
5     }
6     ...
7   
8     class Inner1Thread {
9       class Inner2Thread {
10        int var0;
11        ...
12          // access here
13          var1 = 2; // Error -> Fail
14          var1(2);  // Success -> OK
15        ...
16      }
17    }
18  }
```

Figure 5.24: SAMPEL: Java code example for getter/setter methods accessing local variables

5.2.2.5 Addressing

To ease addressing a specific *AWSM service* with the AWSM platform, an addressing schema was implemented, in which the process name and the target location is sufficient (the specific instance is implicitly specified by the correlation set).

In addition to the *AWSM service* facets, the code generator creates a *proxy Web service*, which is deployed within the Web service container. It is accessible at

<serverURI>/<deploymentPath>/<processname>

The proxy receives all messages for a particular application (corresponds to a SAMPEL description) and routes them to the appropriate *AWSM service* instance specified by the correlation set. Therefore, the generated *AWSM services* contain programme logic that automatically registers and unregisters the particular instance with its `instanceID` at the application proxy.

5.3 Modelling Self-Adaptive Mobile Processes

Overall, generating a fundamentally adaptive application requires the definition of various XML documents. Paired with at least one WSDL description an appropriate SAMPEL description provides the SAMProc adaptation logic. On the basis of this textual representation, the presented code generator is able to generate the necessary application code.

For even simplifying the generation of these XML documents, this thesis introduces an Eclipse plug-in that allows modelling fundamentally adaptive applications with a graphical notation. Since Eclipse already provides a WSDL editor [Ecl09b], the SAMProc plug-in delivers a novel Graphical Modeling Framework (GMF) [Ecl09d] diagram editor that assists application developers in building SAMPEL descriptions. It allows dropping and combining activities on a drawing canvas. During modelling, the editor provides further assistance by validating the structural and semantic correctness of the document.

For initially creating a SAMPEL description that references one or more WSDL documents the application developer is able to use an Eclipse wizard. This wizard allows selecting different templates which serve as scaffolds for common use cases. The created document can be edited in the diagram editor.

The diagram editor is realised with the GMF [Ecl09d], which provides a generative component and runtime infrastructure for graphical editors based on a structured data model (i.e., an Eclipse Modeling Framework (EMF) [Ecl09a] *ecore model* derived from the SAMPEL XML schema). Since GMF separately manages data model, graphical representation and tooling definition, the diagram editor is highly customisable and easy to extend.

Figure 5.25 shows the user interface of the diagram editor. The graphical notation is similar to the Business Process Modelling Notation (BPMN) [OMG09]. Due to the fact that BPMN allows modelling BPEL processes, all SAMPEL elements that are inherited from BPEL are represented with the direct BPMN counterpart. Only for the explicit fundamental adaptation support, new activities were introduced (i.e., move, copy, clone and adapt).

The diagram canvas represents the SAMProc. The palette on the right allows selecting different kinds of tools to edit the process. In particular, there are generation tools for basic and structuring SAMPEL activities (see Section 5.2.1.8 and 5.2.1.9). Basic activities are essential elements of a process and are represented by a rectangular shape with a distinct icon and title. Since structuring activities form the control sequence for basic activities they are represented as titled rectangular containers for nested activities. Due to the fact that each change with respect to

5.3 Modelling Self-Adaptive Mobile Processes

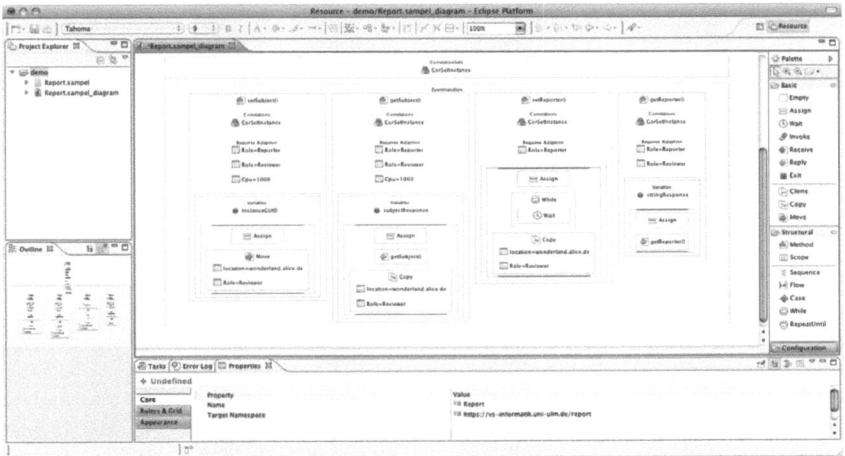

Figure 5.25: SAMPEL diagram editor with a report application model

the data model is performed using the GMF command framework, undo behaviour is seamlessly integrated.

The diagram itself does not display all required information to create a valid document, as this would impair the readability. Therefore, additional information can be captured and edited in the *Eclipse Properties View* by selecting the respective diagram element (see Figure 5.25).

Furthermore, the *Eclipse Problem View* displays errors and warnings that are detected during validation (see Figure 5.26). In addition to structural flaws, such as if a scope has less than one method definition, there are also various semantic correctness constraints with respect to the SAMPEL description. For instance, each process describes its communication endpoints by means of a partner link that must relate to a predefined partner link type of its WSDL description. Those constraints are specified as best practice constraints using the openArchitectureWare Check (oAW-Check) language [ope09], which is straightforward to use. Consequently, constraints can be extended with low efforts.

5 Development Support

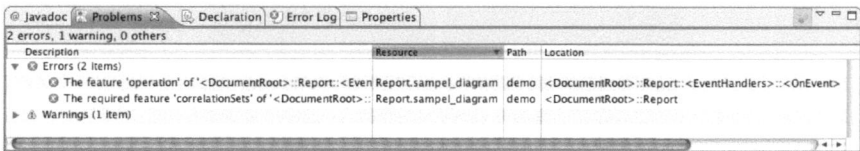

Figure 5.26: SAMPEL editor validation

5.4 Related Work

There is related work in the area of mobile processes. For instance, *Ishikawa et al.* present a framework for mobile Web services, i.e., a synthesis of Web services and mobile agents [ITYH06]. Each mobile Web service has a process description on the basis of BPEL, which is used for interaction with other processes and for supporting migration decisions at runtime. This approach with its BPEL extension has similarities with SAMProcs and SAMPEL. Unlike the approach of this thesis, it does not support fundamental adaptation. Additionally, while the process description of mobile Web services is interpreted at runtime, this thesis introduces SAMPEL for generating code.

Kunze et al. follow a similar approach with DEMAC [KZL06]. There, the process description is a proprietary XML application being executed by the DEMAC process engine at runtime. Instead of using Web service and mobile agent concepts, plain process descriptions are transferred between process engines for achieving mobility. Unlike the DEMAC approach, SAMProcs do not require a pre-installed process execution engine on each device the platform is running. Additionally, the approach of this thesis leads to generated node-tailored code, which makes the SAMProc approach more lightweight at runtime.

There is a lot of research regarding model-driven development of adaptive applications on the basis of distributed component infrastructures. Most of these systems, such as proposed by *MADAM* [GBE+09] and *Phung-Khac et al.* [PKBGS08], allow modelling adaptation (i.e., dynamic component reconfiguration) decisions being executed at runtime. Unlike the approach of this thesis, these frameworks are restricted to a custom component framework and do not support fundamental application adaptation with respect to migration.

Notations such as BPMN [OMG09] define a business process diagram, which is typically a flowchart incorporating constructs suitable for business process analysts and designers. Yet, the graphical notation for SAMPEL reflects the underlying structure of the language with respect to the specific functional oriented design of SAMProcs. This particularly suits application developers by emphasising the control-flow of a fundamentally adaptive application.

5.5 Summary

This chapter showed a model-driven approach to ease the development of fundamentally adaptive applications with *AWSM services*. On the basis of the introduced novel SAMProc abstraction, this thesis proposes SAMPEL, an XML application to describe fundamentally adaptive applications. In contrast to related work, SAMPEL is not interpreted at runtime but used for generating the fundamental adaptation logic for *AWSM services* in such a way that application developers do not have to care about the fundamental adaptation logic anymore. Thus, developers can focus on the pure application logic. Furthermore, this thesis provides a novel Eclipse plug-in to model SAMProc adaptation with a graphical notation. An appropriate SAMPEL description is automatically generated on the basis of the model. This is a major step towards an integrated model-driven development of tailored fundamental adaptive applications on the basis of SAMProcs.

6
Conclusion

This thesis addresses three important problems that arise in the context of mobile and UbiComp application development: support for heterogeneity with respect to migration, strategies to implement fundamental adaptation steps of an application and support for resource-constrained devices.

For supporting heterogeneous migration, this thesis proposes a solution on the basis of an abstract state description that is mapped to environment-specific representations and code for automatic conversion. In addition, a service for the dynamic management of platform-specific code even enables migration to locations where the necessary code is unavailable. A context service and a service for entity discovery support migration decisions.

With respect to the implementation of fundamentally adaptive applications, this thesis introduces a solution supporting the developer by separating the adaptation from the application logic. There, model-driven development (MDD) techniques allow generating the fundamental adaptation logic from an abstract application description. The aforementioned context service supports adaptation decisions at runtime.

Regarding the support of resource-constrained devices, this thesis presents a solution that minimises memory usage. It introduces concepts for minimising the data necessary for execution

6 *Conclusion*

and loading tailored code on demand. The lean Soap*ME* Web service container contributes to this.

6.1 Main Contributions

The proposed AXM infrastructure is a novel architectural design pattern for developing fundamentally adaptive applications in mobile and UbiComp scenarios. Unlike related work, AXM supports fundamental adaptation of an application in terms of the available state, provided functionality, implementation in use and the current location (i.e., migration), while even supporting dynamic and heterogeneous environments. Moreover, AXM is independent of the concrete implementation infrastructure and platform: this thesis presents two prototypes, the CORBA-based AOM system and the Web-service–based AWSM platform. The evaluation of the prototypes in typical mobile and UbiComp scenarios shows that the AXM implementation platform has a high impact on the performance. Yet, both prototypes show reasonable performance for most scenarios. Only the evaluation settings with the Nokia N810 device running Java as target platform provide weak performance. Yet, the evaluation also shows that using C++ as an alternative target platform on the N810 considerably improves performance. Moreover, an AWSM prototype on the basis of Soap*ME* could further improve performance in this setting.

This thesis introduces several services supporting applications in mobile and UbiComp scenarios, such as *dynamic code management* (DCM). This is a highly relevant service in such highly dynamic scenarios because implementation code cannot be preinstalled on all relevant devices in advance. DCM offers a generic concept for centralised and decentralised sharing, discovering, selecting, and deploying of platform-specific code on demand. There are prototype implementations for Java and OSGi on the basis of JXTA. The OSGi prototype is part of the AWSM platform. Unlike related work, functional as well as non-functional properties are considered during the discovery and selection process. Moreover, DCM allows automatic resolution of implementation code dependencies on the basis of functional and non-functional properties.

The generic context service supports run-time decisions with respect to fundamental application adaptation. Unlike related work, it specifies a generic context model and is implemented with standards only, such as OWL for describing and SPARQL for querying and monitoring context. Moreover, it builds up a highly modular architecture that allows adding context components and their sensors at runtime. The service is accessible by a standard Web service interface, which eases the integration with available mobile and UbiComp infrastructures, such as AWSM.

SoapME is a lightweight and very flexible Web service container for Java ME CLDC. The design and the prototype implementation with a code size of only about 200kB particularly support resource-limited devices and provide communication for mobile and UbiComp platforms, such as AWSM. SoapME is the first Web service container for Java ME CLDC providing dynamic deployment and reasonable performance on a mobile device.

This thesis introduces a novel service to discover entities, such as users, devices and services with given characteristics. It is implemented on the basis of SIP, the common session management protocol for next generation mobile phone networks. Thus, it provides an alternative to the context service in scenarios with devices having access to such networks. Unlike state-of-the-art approaches, it requires no separate infrastructure for entity discovery. This reduces overall network complexity and requires no separate entity discovery client on the mobile device. Due to the fact that standard SIP infrastructure is centralised and thus cannot be assumed working in typical mobile and UbiComp scenarios, a decentralised approach on the basis of JXTA was developed. Unlike related work, it offers SIP compliance, allows using arbitrary P2P mechanisms and integrates entity discovery.

Even with middleware support, such as proposed with the AXM-based prototypes, developing fundamentally adaptive applications is still a non-trivial task. Thus, this thesis suggests model-driven development of fundamentally adaptive applications on the basis of the novel *self-adaptive mobile process* (SAMProc) concept. A SAMProc supports an abstract application specification that is independent from the underlying technology and the dynamic and heterogeneous infrastructure. For this purpose, SAMPEL is introduced as a novel XML application to describe fundamentally adaptive applications on the basis of the SAMProc abstraction. Unlike related work, SAMPEL is not interpreted at runtime but used for generating the fundamental adaptation logic for *AWSM services*. Application developers do not have to implement the fundamental adaptation logic; they can focus on the pure application logic. In addition, an Eclipse plug-in allows modelling SAMProcs. On the basis of a graphical notation it automatically generates the appropriate SAMPEL description. Thus, it offers developers an integrated approach to implement fundamentally adaptive applications in a model-driven way.

6.2 Limitations and Future Work

The AXM prototypes show reasonable performance on devices used in the introduced mobile and UbiComp scenarios. Yet, for the AWSM Java prototype running on the resource-limited N810 Internet tablet performance is poor. Thus, AWSM should be implemented on top of future mobile Web service containers to improve this performance bottleneck. The author does not expect interoperability problems, as the infrastructure is designed to rely on standard Web service technology only. AWSM requires only interceptors and dynamic deployment at the Web service container. In future work, one could also investigate the CORBA/e standard for embedded systems [OMG06] to implement AOM. CORBA/e specifies a *compact profile* that supports CORBA value types. This allows transferring the AOM concept to embedded devices. Yet, due to the fact that the CORBA/e standard does not support many dynamic features of standard CORBA the concept has to be adapted to new requirements (e.g., CORBA/e does not support the interface repository and the dynamic invocation interface).

Moreover, AXM provides a very generic concept to implement fundamentally adaptive applications. In possible future work, other concepts and platforms could build the basis to implement this architectural design pattern, for instance using components [Szy02] or the .NET platform [Mic09].

The DCM platform does not allow the publication of more than one interface per resource (i.e., standalone implementation code or OSGi bundle). Yet, as resources may provide more than one interface, the resource publication mechanism should be extended. Moreover, the author argued for the necessity of supporting non-functional properties. For handling these properties in larger systems, support for ontologies describing non-functional properties is necessary. This can also build the basis to implement enhanced matching of dependencies using semantic discovery approaches. Furthermore, the DCM infrastructure already provides a basis for application deployment with a given blueprint. This blueprint information can be used to select, load and deploy tailored implementations providing the required service functionality with the DCM infrastructure. An enhancement of such a simple blueprint mechanism—a sophisticated distributed application deployment platform—could be subject to future work.

The context service already supports essential run-time decisions of fundamentally adaptive applications. Yet, it could be improved with probabilistic context support and further development tools. In particular, writing SPARQL queries for specifying required context is complex. Thus, a tool could be developed, which allows browsing context ontologies and modelling the required context profile with this information. This tool could be part of the presented Eclipse modelling plug-in to generate appropriate SPARQL queries.

Soap*ME* is a fully-fledged Web service container for Java ME CLDC. Yet, possible future work could be supporting Web service discovery via Bluetooth in order to achieve a more integrated infrastructure, which could rely on Bluetooth only. Furthermore, the architecture could be revised with respect to distribution. In a typical mobile and UbiComp scenario with a lot of resource-limited devices, parts of the infrastructure, such as the Web service proxy, could be installed on powerful gateways, such as proposed by *Srirama et al.* [SJP07].

In the proposed P2P SIP approach, requests are not forwarded via the target's home-domain proxy anymore. This results in a reduction of session establishment time but leads to a potential issue as home-domain proxies may be used for resource reservation purposes [TIS08]. Yet, this matter can be solved by introducing a mechanism into the approach to forward requests via the home-domain proxy of the target if needed. Thus, at least proxies in the proxy-chain between the sender's home-domain proxy and the target's home-domain proxy can be skipped, which also leads to an improved time for session establishment in comparison to standard SIP. Moreover, the evaluation could be broadened by replacing the standard JXTA routing protocol with different P2P protocols, such as protocols that are suitable for mobile networks. Finally, to gain more realistic results, an evaluation with more senders and receivers in a real world setting, for instance using PlanetLab [PACR03], could be subject to future work.

The SAMProc abstraction provides basic means to describe fundamentally adaptive applications. Still, one could investigate advanced mechanisms for SAMProcs. Amongst others, these could be feedback mechanisms within the SAMProc, exception handling and means for cloning and merging SAMProcs (e.g., on the basis of the fragmented object model [KDH$^+$06]).

The model-driven approach eases developing fundamentally adaptive applications on the basis of the SAMProc concept. Yet, if an application has many adaptation cases, the code generation tool creates a lot of facets. For supporting the developer by generating as much code as possible one could investigate the direct annotation of custom SAMPEL activities with program code in the model. Such an approach is similar to *BPELJ* [BGK$^+$04], which allows using Java code within BPEL. Moreover, although personal feedback regarding the simplification of application development was throughout positive, a quantitative evaluation with two groups of developers implementing the same application could support this impression (one group uses SAMProc the other does not).

With the AXM-compliant prototypes, the infrastructure services and the model-driven approach to application development, this thesis fulfils all requirements of Section 2.3. Yet, these requirements were determined by analysing a rather small set of applications. Although these applications represent a broad set of typical mobile and UbiComp applications, new applications might have further requirements. Yet, due to the fact that the infrastructure and all infrastructure services were designed and implemented with a strong focus on using available standards they should be extensible with low efforts.

6 Conclusion

This thesis introduces a novel programming model of an application that is able to fundamentally adapt in terms of interface, state, implementation and location. To build up a broad acceptance of such a novel programming model, future work should investigate further applications scenarios. For instance, SAMProcs could be used to autonomously collect data in sensor networks, to implement a surveillance application that follows a user and even to support the field staff of a company with local business process support. Moreover, the software that was developed as part of this thesis has been deployed in rather small settings so far. To gain a more realistic experience these applications should be deployed in real-life scenarios and be evaluated by a high number of users over a long period of time. The results of such an evaluation should lead to an improved understanding of user requirements in mobile and UbiComp scenarios. Such an understanding can be used to improve the AXM-based prototypes and their supportive services.

Bibliography

[3GP09] 3GPP, *IP multimedia subsystem (IMS); stage 2 (release 9)*, TS 23.228, 3GPP, June 2009.

[Act09] Active Endpoints, *ActiveBPEL open source engine project*, <http://www.active-endpoints.com>, 2009.

[Ada05] C. Adamson, *Quick time for Java: A developer's notebook*, O'Reilly Media, Inc., January 2005.

[AE08] V. Abu-Eid, *Running Axis2 in OSGi environments*, <http://www.dynamicjava.org/posts/running-axis2-in-osgi>, September 2008.

[AEHS06] M. Alia, F. Eliassen, S. Hallsteinsen, and E. Stav, *Madam: Towards a flexible planning-based middleware (extended abstract)*, SEAMS '06: ICSE 2006 Workshop on Software Engineering for Adaptive and Self-Managing Systems, May 2006.

[Apa06] Apache Software Foundation, *Axis*, <http://ws.apache.org/axis/>, 2006.

[Apa09a] _____, *Apache Felix*, <http://felix.apache.org/>, 2009.

[Apa09b] _____, *Apache Tomcat*, <http://tomcat.apache.org/>, 2009.

[AWvSN01] J. Almeida, M. Wegdam, M. van Sinderen, and L. Nieuwenhuis, *Transparent dynamic reconfiguration for CORBA*, DOA '01: 3rd International Symposium on Distributed Objects and Applications, IEEE Computer Society, September 2001, pp. 197–207.

[Bar03] D. K. Barry, *Web services and service-oriented architectures*, Elsevier, April 2003.

[BCF+06] W. Binder, I. Constantinescu, B. Faltings, K. Haller, and C. Türker, *A multiagent system for the reliable execution of automatically composed ad-hoc processes*, Journal of Autonomous Agents and Multi-Agent Systems **12** (2006), no. 2, 219–237.

[BCS00]   P. Bellavista, A. Corradi, and C. Stefanelli, *CORBA solutions for interoperability in mobile agent environments*, DOA '00: 2nd International Symposium on Distributed Objects and Applications, IEEE Computer Society, September 2000, pp. 283–292.

[BGK+04] M. Blow, Y. Goland, M. Kloppmann, F. Leymann, G. Pfau, D. Roller, and M. Rowley, *BPELJ: BPEL for Java*, White paper, March 2004.

[BHR01]   R. Brandt, C. Hörtnagel, and H. Reiser, *Dynamically adaptable mobile agents for scaleable software and service management*, Journal of Communications and Networks (JCN) **3** (2001), no. 4, 307–316.

[BHRS98] J. Baumann, F. Hohl, K. Rothermel, and M. Strasser, *Mole – concepts of a mobile agent system*, World Wide Web (WWW) **1** (1998), no. 3, 123–137.

[BHSR04] C. Becker, M. Handte, G. Schiele, and K. Rothermel, *PCOM - a component system for pervasive computing*, PerCom '04: 2nd IEEE International Conference on Pervasive Computing and Communications, IEEE Computer Society, March 2004, p. 67.

[BL07]   D. A. Bryan and B. B. Lowekamp, *Decentralizing SIP*, ACM Queue **5** (2007), no. 2, 34–41.

[BLJ07]   D. A. Bryan, B. B. Lowekamp, and C. Jennings, *dSIP: A P2P approach to SIP registration and resource location*, IETF Internet-Draft draft-bryan-p2psip-dsip-00, February 2007.

[BOvSW02] F. M. T. Brazier, B. J. Overeinder, M. van Steen, and N. J. E. Wijngaards, *Agent factory: generative migration of mobile agents in heterogeneous environments*, SAC '02: ACM symposium on Applied computing, ACM, March 2002, pp. 101–106.

[BR00]   R. Brandt and H. Reiser, *Dynamic adaptation of mobile agents in heterogenous environments*, MA '01: 5th International Conference on Mobile Agents, Lecture Notes in Computer Science, vol. 2240, December 2000, pp. 70–87.

[BSGR03] C. Becker, G. Schiele, H. Gubbels, and K. Rothermel, *BASE - a micro-broker-based middleware for pervasive computing*, PerCom '03: IEEE International Conference on Pervasive Computing and Communications, IEEE Computer Society, March 2003.

[BSN05]   M. Brunner, M. Stiemerling, and S. Niccolini, *Requirements and framework for SIP user agent auto-configuration*, IETF Internet-Draft draft-brunner-sipping-sipautoconf-00, October 2005.

[BSSW03] S. Berger, H. Schulzrinne, S. Sidiroglou, and X. Wu, *Ubiquitous computing using SIP*, NOSSDAV '03: International Workshop on Network and Operating System Support for Digital Audio and Video, June 2003.

[CBM99] S. Choy, M. Breugst, and T. Magedanz, *A CORBA environment supporting mobile objects*, IS&N '99: 6th International Conference on Intelligence and Services in Networks, Lecture Notes In Computer Science, vol. 1597, Springer, April 1999, pp. 168–180.

[CDF+07] J. Callas, L. Donnerhacke, H. Finney, D. Shaw, and F. Thayer, *OpenPGP message format*, IETF RFC 4880, November 2007.

[CFH+05] C. Clark, K. Fraser, S. Hand, J. G. Hansen, E. Jul, C. Limpach, I. Pratt, and A. Warfield, *Live migration of virtual machines*, NSDI '05: 2nd ACM/USENIX Symposium on Networked Systems Design and Implementation, May 2005, pp. 273–286.

[CR02] J. Coutaz and G. Rey, *Foundations for a theory of contextors*, CADUI '02: 4th International Conference on Computer-Aided Design of User Interfaces, Kluwer, May 2002.

[CSF+08] D. Cooper, S. Santesson, S. Farrell, S. Boeyen, R. Housley, and W. Polk, *Internet X.509 public key infrastructure certificate and certificate revocation list (CRL) profile*, IETF RFC 5280, May 2008.

[DAS99] A. K. Dey, G. D. Abowd, and D. Salber, *A context-based infrastructure for smart environments*, MANSE '99: 1st International Workshop on Managing Interactions in Smart Environments, Springer, December 1999.

[Dey01] A. K. Dey, *Understanding and using context*, Personal and Ubiquitous Computing (PUC) **5** (2001), no. 1, 4–7.

[Dik06] J. Dike, *User mode Linux*, Prentice Hall, April 2006.

[dRE06] R. A. da Rocha and M. Endler, *Middleware: Context management in heterogeneous, evolving ubiquitous environments*, IEEE Distributed Systems Online (DSOnline) **7** (2006), no. 4, 1.

[DvCM+05] J. Dedecker, T. van Cutsem, S. Mostinckx, T. D'Hondt, and W. de Meuter, *Ambient-oriented programming*, OOPSLA '05, ACM Press, October 2005, pp. 31–40.

Bibliography

[DWFB97] N. Davies, S. P. Wade, A. Friday, and G. S. Blair, *Limbo: a tuple space based platform for adaptive mobile applications*, ICODP/ICDP '97: Proceedings of the IFIP/IEEE international conference on Open distributed processing and distributed platforms, Chapman & Hall, Ltd., May 1997, pp. 291–302.

[Ecl09a] Eclipse Foundation, *Eclipse modeling framework*, <http://www.eclipse.org/emf>, 2009.

[Ecl09b] _____, *Eclipse Web tools platform*, <http://www.eclipse.org/wtp>, 2009.

[Ecl09c] _____, *Equinox*, <http://www.eclipse.org/equinox/>, 2009.

[Ecl09d] _____, *Graphical modeling framework*, <http://www.eclipse.org/gmf>, 2009.

[EG02] R. A. Van Engelen and K. A. Gallivan, *The gSOAP toolkit for Web services and peer-to-peer computing networks*, CCGrid '02: 2nd IEEE/ACM International Symposium on Cluster Computing and the Grid, May 2002.

[Elo08] J. Elonen, *NanoHTTPD*, <http://elonen.iki.fi/code/nanohttpd/>, April 2008.

[ESZK04] J. Eberspächer, R. Schollmeier, S. Zöls, and G. Kunzmann, *Structured P2P networks in mobile and fixed environments*, HET-NETs '04: International Working Conference on Performance Modelling and Evaluation of Heterogeneous Networks, July 2004.

[ETM07] A. Erradi, V. Tosic, and P. Maheshwari, *MASC - .NET-based middleware for adaptive composite Web services*, ICWS '07: International Conference on Web Services, July 2007, pp. 727–734.

[ETS94] ETSI, *ETSI ETS 300 509 European digital cellular telecommunications system (phase 2); subscriber identity modules (SIM) functional characteristics*, Technical Specification, January 1994.

[EY04] J. Ellis and M. Young, *J2ME Web services 1.0*, JSR 172, March 2004.

[FPV98] A. Fuggetta, G. P. Picco, and G. Vigna, *Understanding code mobility*, IEEE Transactions on Software Engineering (TOSE) **24** (1998), no. 5, 342–361.

[FR05] S. Frenot and Y. Royon, *Component deployment using a peer-to-peer overlay*, CD '05: Proceedings of the 3rd International Working Conference on Component Deployment, Lecture Notes in Computer Science, vol. 3798, 2005.

[FS03] N. Ferguson and B. Schneier, *Practical Cryptography*, Wiley & Sons, March 2003.

[FV09]　K. Fall and K. Varadhan, *The ns manual (formerly ns notes and documentation)*, <http://www.isi.edu/nsnam/ns/doc/ns_doc.pdf>, January 2009.

[GBE+09]　K. Geihs, P. Barone, F. Eliassena, J. Floch, R. Fricke, E. Gjorven, S. Hallsteinsen, G. Horn, M. Khan, A. Mamelli, G. Papadopoulos, N. Paspallis, R. Reichle, and E. Stav, *A comprehensive solution for application-level adaptation*, Software: Practice and Experience (SPE) **39** (2009), no. 4, 385–422.

[GCK+02]　R. S. Gray, G. Cybenko, D. Kotz, R. A. Peterson, and D. Rus, *D'Agents: Applications and performance of a mobile-agent system*, Software: Practice and Experience (SPE) **32** (2002), no. 6, 543–573.

[Gel85]　D. Gelernter, *Generative communication in Linda*, ACM Transactions on Programming Languages and Systems (TOPLAS) **7** (1985), no. 1, 80–112.

[GGH+05]　B. Garbinato, R. Guerraoui, J. Hulaas, O. L. Madsen, M. Monod, and J. H. Spring, *Mobile computing with frugal objects*, Tech. report, EPFL I&C, July 2005.

[GGH+07]　B. Garbinato, R. Guerraoui, J. Hulaas, M. Monod, and J. H. Spring, *Pervasive computing with frugal objects*, AINAW '07: 21st International Conference on Advanced Information Networking and Applications Workshops, IEEE Computer Society, May 2007, pp. 13–18.

[GHJV95]　E. Gamma, R. Helm, R. Johnson, and J. Vlissides, *Design patterns: Elements of reusable object-oriented languages and systems*, Addison-Wesley, March 1995.

[GLK04]　T. Guenkova-Luy and A. Kassler, *End-to-end quality of service coordination for multimedia applications in heterogeneous, mobile networks*, ICC '04: IEEE International Conference on Communications, June 2004.

[GLKM04]　T. Guenkova-Luy, A. Kassler, and D. Mandato, *End-to-end quality of service coordination for multimedia applications*, IEEE Journal on Selected Areas in Communications (JSAC) **22** (2004), no. 5, 889–903.

[GLSH+06]　T. Guenkova-Luy, A. Schorr, F. Hauck, M. Gomez, C. Timmerer, I. Wolf, and A. Kassler, *Advanced multimedia management - control model and content adaptation*, EuroIMSA '06: IASTED International Conference on Internet and Multimedia Systems and Applications, February 2006.

[Gon01]　L. Gong, *JXTA: A network programming environment*, IEEE Internet Computing (IC) **5** (2001), no. 3, 88–95.

Bibliography

[GPVD99] E. Guttman, C. Perkins, J. Veizades, and M. Day, *Service location protocol, version 2*, IETF RFC 2608, June 1999.

[HIR03] K. Henricksen, J. Indulska, and A. Rakotonirainy, *Generating context management infrastructure from high-level context models*, MDM '03: 4th International Conference on Mobile Data Management, Industrial Track Proceedings, January 2003.

[HJ98] M. Handley and V. Jacobson, *SDP: Session description protocol*, IETF RFC 2327, April 1998.

[HL06] B. C. Hammerschmidt and V. Linnemann, *Migratable Web services: Increasing performance and privacy in service oriented architectures*, IADIS International Journal on Computer Science and Information Systems **1** (2006), no. 1, 42–56.

[IRRH03] J. Indulska, R. Robinson, A. Rakotonirainy, and K. Henricksen, *Experiences in using CC/PP in context-aware systems*, MDM '03: 4th International Conference on Mobile Data Management, Springer, January 2003, pp. 247–261.

[ITU04] ITU, *General overview of NGN*, ITU-T Recommendation Y.2001, December 2004.

[ITYH06] F. Ishikawa, Y. Tahara, N. Yoshioka, and S. Honiden, *Formal model of mobile BPEL4WS process*, International Journal of Business Process Integration and Management (IJBPIM) **1** (2006), no. 3, 192–209.

[IYTH04] F. Ishikawa, N. Yoshioka, Y. Tahara, and S. Honiden, *Mobile agent system for Web services integration in pervasive networks*, IWUC '04: International Workshop on Ubiquitous Computing, April 2004, pp. 38–47.

[JLHB88] E. Jul, H. Levy, N. Hutchinson, and A. Black, *Fine-grained mobility in the Emerald system*, ACM Transactions on Computer Systems (TOCS) **6** (1988), no. 1, 109–133.

[JLR+09a] C. Jennings, B. Lowekamp, E. Rescorla, S. Baset, and H. Schulzrinne, *REsource LOcation And Discovery (RELOAD) base protocol*, IETF Internet-Draft draft-ietf-p2psip-base-03, July 2009.

[JLR+09b] _____, *A SIP usage for RELOAD*, IETF Internet-Draft draft-ietf-p2psip-sip-01, March 2009.

[JSR06] JSR 118 Expert Group, *Mobile Information Device Profile for Java 2 Micro Edition Version 2.0*, JSR 118, June 2006.

[KDH+06] R. Kapitza, J. Domaschka, F. J. Hauck, H. P. Reiser, and H. Schmidt, *FORMI: Integrating adaptive fragmented objects into Java RMI*, IEEE Distributed Systems Online (DSOnline) **7** (2006), no. 10, 1.

[KH03] R. Kapitza and F.J. Hauck, *DLS: a CORBA service for dynamic loading of code*, On The Move to Meaningful Internet Systems 2003: CoopIS, DOA, and ODBASE, November 2003.

[KSBH07] R. Kapitza, H. Schmidt, U. Bartlang, and F. J. Hauck, *A generic infrastructure for decentralised dynamic loading of platform-specific code*, DAIS '07: 7th International Conference on Distributed Applications and Interoperable Systems, Lecture Notes in Computer Science, vol. 4531, June 2007, pp. 323–336.

[KSH05] R. Kapitza, H. Schmidt, and F. J. Hauck, *Platform-independent object migration in CORBA*, On the Move to Meaningful Internet Systems 2005: CoopIS, DOA, and ODBASE, Lecture Notes in Computer Science, vol. 3760, October 2005, pp. 900–917.

[KSSH06] R. Kapitza, H. Schmidt, G. Söldner, and F. J. Hauck, *A framework for adaptive mobile objects in heterogeneous environments*, On the Move to Meaningful Internet Systems 2006: CoopIS, DOA, GADA, and ODBASE (Robert Meersman and Zahir Tari, eds.), Lecture Notes in Computer Science, vol. 4276, Springer, October 2006, pp. 1739–1756.

[KZL06] C. P. Kunze, S. Zaplata, and W. Lamersdorf, *Mobile process description and execution*, DAIS '06: 6th International Conference on Distributed Applications and Interoperable Systems, Lecture Notes in Computer Science, vol. 4025, June 2006, pp. 32–47.

[Lag09] B. Lagesse, *Trust and security in dynamic systems*, PERCOM '09: IEEE International Conference on Pervasive Computing and Communications, IEEE Computer Society, March 2009.

[Lev98] E. Levinson, *The MIME multipart/related content-type*, IETF RFC 2387, August 1998.

[LJP06] I. Lera, C. Juiz, and R. Puigjaner, *Performance-related ontologies for ubiquitous intelligence based on semantic Web applications*, AINA '06: Proceedings of the 20th International Conference on Advanced Information Networking and Applications - Volume 1, IEEE Computer Society, April 2006, pp. 675–682.

Bibliography

[LKNZ08] L. Luo, A. Kansal, S. Nath, and F. Zhao, *Sharing and exploring sensor streams over geocentric interfaces*, GIS '08: 16th ACM SIGSPATIAL international conference on Advances in geographic information systems, ACM, November 2008, pp. 1–10.

[LO98] D. B. Lange and M. Oshima, *Programming and deploying Java mobile agents with Aglets*, Addison-Wesley, August 1998.

[Mar09] M. Marrone, *Twitter grabs spotlight with Janis Krums' US Airways crash photo, then won't shut up about it*, NY Daily News, January 2009.

[MBB+99] D. Milojičić, M. Breugst, I. Busse, J. Campbell, S. Covaci, B. Friedman, K. Kosaka, D. Lange, K. Ono, M. Oshima, C. Tham, S. Virdhagriswaran, and J. White, *MASIF, the OMG mobile agent system interoperability facility*, Mobility: processes, computers, and agents, ACM Press/Addison-Wesley Publishing Co., April 1999, pp. 628–641.

[Mic06] Microsoft Corporation, *Devices profile for Web services*, February 2006.

[Mic09] _____, *.NET framework developer center*, <http://msdn.microsoft.com/netframework/>, 2009.

[MJ98] D. Mosberger and T. Jin, *httperf–a tool for measuring Web server performance*, SIGMETRICS Performance Evaluation Review (PER) **26** (1998), no. 3, 31–37.

[MLC98] D. Milojičić, W. LaForge, and D. Chauhan, *Mobile objects and agents (MOA)*, COOTS '98: 4th USENIX Conference on Object-Oriented Technologies and Systems, April 1998, pp. 179–194.

[MM99] C. A. Mendez and M. Mendes, *Agent migration issues in CORBA platforms*, ISADS '99: 5th International Symposium on Autonomous Decentralized Systems, March 1999.

[Mot09] Motorola, Inc., *Mobile information device profile for Java micro edition, version 3.0*, JSR 271, May 2009.

[Nec97] G. C. Necula, *Proof-carrying code*, POPL '97: The 24th ACM SIGPLAN-SIGACT Symposium on Principles of Programming Languages, January 1997, pp. 106–119.

[Net02] Network Working Group, *(extensible markup language) XML-signature syntax and processing*, IETF RFC 3275, March 2002.

[NIS09] NIST, *jain-sip: Java API for SIP signaling*, <https://jain-sip.dev.java.net/>, 2009.

[NTM01]   J. Noble, A. Taivalsaari, and I. Moore (eds.), *Prototype-based programming: Concepts, languages and applications*, Springer, January 2001.

[OAS04]   OASIS, *Introduction to UDDI: Important features and functional concepts*, White paper, October 2004.

[OAS06]   _____, *Web services security: SOAP message security 1.1*, February 2006.

[OAS07]   _____, *Web services business process execution language version 2.0*, April 2007.

[OMG02]   OMG, *Life cycle service specification*, OMG Document formal/2002-09-01, September 2002.

[OMG03]   _____, *MDA guide version 1.0.1*, OMG Doc. omg/2003-06-01, June 2003.

[OMG04a] _____, *Common object request broker architecture*, OMG Document formal/2004-03-12, March 2004.

[OMG04b] _____, *Naming service specification*, OMG Document formal/2004-10-03, October 2004.

[OMG06]   _____, *CORBA/e draft adopted specification*, OMG document ptc/06-05-01, May 2006.

[OMG09]   _____, *Business process modeling notation (BPMN), version 1.2*, OMG Document formal/2009-01-03, January 2009.

[ON98]   P. D. O'Brien and R. C. Nicol, *FIPA — towards a standard for software agents*, BT Technology Journal **16** (1998), no. 3, 51–59.

[ope09]   openArchitectureWare.org, *openarchitectureware*, <http://www.openarchitectureware.org>, 2009.

[Ort03]   E. Ortiz, *The MIDP 2.0 push registry*, Sun Developer Network, January 2003.

[OSG06]   OSGi Alliance, *RFC-0112 bundle repository*, February 2006.

[OSG07a] _____, *OSGi service platform: Core specification, release 4, version 4.1*, May 2007.

[OSG07b] _____, *OSGi service platform: Service compendium, release 4, version 4.1*, May 2007.

[OSG09]   _____, *OSGi service platform: Service compendium, release 4, version 4.2*, September 2009.

Bibliography

[PACR03] L. Peterson, T. Anderson, D. Culler, and T. Roscoe, *A blueprint for introducing disruptive technology into the Internet*, SIGCOMM Computer Communication Review (CCR) **33** (2003), no. 1, 59–64.

[PC03] D. Parker and D. Cleary, *A P2P approach to ClassLoading in Java*, AP2PC '03: 2nd International Workshop on Agents and Peer-to-Peer Computing, July 2003.

[PG00] Y. Peter and H. Guyennet, *Object mobility in large scale systems*, Cluster Computing **3** (2000), no. 2, 177–185.

[PKBGS08] A. Phung-Khac, A. Beugnard, J.-M. Gilliot, and M.-T. Segarra, *Model-driven development of component-based adaptive distributed applications*, SAC '08: Symposium on Applied Computing, ACM, March 2008, pp. 2186–2191.

[PKF05] S. Paal, R. Kammüller, and B. Freisleben, *Dynamic software deployment with distributed application repositories*, KiVS '05: 14. Fachtagung Kommunikation in Verteilten Systemen, Springer, February 2005.

[Pro08] Progress Software Corporation, *Orbacus technical review*, White paper, 2008.

[RA07] J. S. Rellermeyer and G. Alonso, *Concierge: a service platform for resource-constrained devices*, SIGOPS Operating Systems Review (OSR) **41** (2007), no. 3, 245–258.

[RAMC+04] A. Ranganathan, J. Al-Muhtadi, S. Chetan, R. Campbell, and M. D. Mickunas, *MiddleWhere: a middleware for location awareness in ubiquitous computing applications*, Middleware '04: 5th ACM/IFIP/USENIX international conference on Middleware, Springer, October 2004.

[Ree79] T. Reenskaug, *Models - Views - Controllers*, Technical note, Xerox PARC, December 1979.

[RGK+05] S. Rhea, B. Godfrey, B. Karp, J. Kubiatowicz, S. Ratnasamy, S. Shenker, I. Stoica, and H. Yu, *OpenDHT: a public DHT service and its uses*, SIGCOMM '05: Proceedings of the 2005 conference on Applications, technologies, architectures, and protocols for computer communications, ACM, August 2005, pp. 73–84.

[RGRK03] S. Rhea, D. Geels, T. Roscoe, and J. Kubiatowicz, *Handling churn in a DHT*, Technical report UCB//CSD-03-1299, University of California, Berkeley, December 2003.

[RS02] J. Rosenberg and H. Schulzrinne, *Session initiation protocol (SIP): Locating SIP servers*, IETF RFC 3263, June 2002.

[RSC+02] J. Rosenberg, H. Schulzrinne, G. Camarillo, A. Johnston, J. Peterson, R. Sparks, M. Handley, and E. Schooler, *SIP: Session initiation protocol*, RFC 3261, June 2002.

[SAT+99] A. Schmidt, K. A. Aidoo, A. Takaluoma, U. Tuomela, K. van Laerhoven, and W. van de Velde, *Advanced interaction in context*, HUC '99: 1st international symposium on Handheld and Ubiquitous Computing, Lecture Notes in Computer Science, vol. 1707, Springer, September 1999.

[Sat01] M. Satyanarayanan, *Pervasive computing: vision and challenges*, IEEE Personal Communications (PCI) **8** (2001), no. 4, 10–17.

[Sat05] I. Satoh, *Network processing of documents, for documents, by documents*, Middleware '05, Lecture Notes in Computer Science, vol. 3790, November 2005, pp. 421–430.

[Sat06] _____, *A document-centric component framework for document distributions*, On the Move to Meaningful Internet Systems 2006: CoopIS, DOA, GADA, and ODBASE, Lecture Notes in Computer Science, vol. 4276, October 2006, pp. 1555–1575.

[SAW94] B. Schilit, N. Adams, and R. Want, *Context-aware computing applications*, WMCSA '94: 1st Workshop on Mobile Computing Systems and Applications, IEEE Computer Society, December 1994.

[SBH97] M. Strasser, J. Baumann, and F. Hohl, *Mole: A Java based mobile agent system*, 2nd ECOOP Workshop on Mobile Object Systems, June 1997.

[Sch96] W. Schulte, *'Service oriented' architectures, part 2*, SSA research note SPA-401-069, Gartner, April 1996.

[Sch02] H. Schulzrinne, *Dynamic host configuration protocol (DHCP-for-IPv4) option for session initiation protocol (SIP) servers*, IETF RFC 3361, 2002.

[Sev99] J. Sevanto, *Multimedia messaging service for GPRS and UMTS*, WCNC '99: Wireless Communications and Networking Conference, vol. 3, IEEE Computer Society, September 1999, pp. 1422–1426.

[SJ95] B. Steensgaard and E. Jul, *Object and native code thread mobility among heterogeneous computers*, SOSP '95: 15th ACM symposium on operating systems principles, ACM, December 1995, pp. 68–77.

Bibliography

[SJP06] S. N. Srirama, M. Jarke, and W. Prinz, *Mobile Web service provisioning*, AICT/ICIW '06: Advanced International Conference on Telecommunications and International Conference on Internet and Web Applications and Services, IEEE Computer Society, February 2006.

[SJP07] _____, *Mobile Web services mediation framework*, MW4SOC '07: Workshop on Middleware for Service Oriented Computing, ACM, November 2007.

[SKHR08] H. Schmidt, R. Kapitza, F. J. Hauck, and H. P. Reiser, *Adaptive Web service migration*, DAIS '08: Distributed Applications and Interoperable Systems, Lecture Notes in Computer Science, vol. 5053, Springer, June 2008, pp. 182–195.

[Sky09] Skype Limited, *Skype*, <http://www.skype.com>, 2009.

[SLPF03] T. Strang, C. Linnhoff-Popien, and K. Frank, *CoOL: A context ontology language to enable contextual interoperability*, DAIS '03: Distributed Applications and Interoperable Systems, LNCS, vol. 2893, Springer, November 2003.

[SMK+03] I. Stoica, R. Morris, D. Karger, F. Kaashoek, and H. Balakrishnan, *Chord: A scalable peer-to-peer lookup service for Internet applications*, IEEE/ACM Transactions on Networking (TON) **11** (2003), no. 1, 17–32.

[SN96] W. Schulte and Y. V. Natis, *'Service oriented' architectures, part 1*, SSA research note SPA-401-068, Gartner, April 1996.

[SOA08] SOA4D Forge, *DPWS4J core*, <https://forge.soa4d.org/projects/dpws4j/>, 2008.

[Sou06a] SourceForge, *JME SOAP server*, <http://sourceforge.net/projects/jmesoapserver/>, 2006.

[Sou06b] _____, *kSOAP 2*, <http://ksoap2.sourceforge.net/>, 2006.

[SS05] K. Singh and H. Schulzrinne, *Peer-to-peer Internet telephony using SIP*, NOSSDAV '05: International Workshop on Network and Operating System Support for Digital Audio and Video, June 2005.

[SS06] _____, *Using an external DHT as a SIP location service*, Technical report CUCS-007-06, Columbia University, February 2006.

[SU95] R. B. Smith and D. Ungar, *Programming as an experience: The inspiration for Self*, ECOOP '95: 9th European Conference on Object-Oriented Programming, August 1995.

[Sun02]   Sun Microsystems, *Java media framework API (JMF) specification, version 2.1.1*, JSR 920, 2002.

[Sun05a] _____, *Java object serialization specification*, <http://java.sun.com/javase/6/docs/platform/serialization/spec/serialTOC.html>, 2005.

[Sun05b] _____, *Java Web start overview*, White paper, May 2005.

[Sun06a] _____, *Connected device configuration 1.1.2*, JSR 218, August 2006.

[Sun06b] _____, *The Java architecture for XML binding (JAXB) 2.0*, JSR 222, May 2006.

[Sun06c] _____, *Java management extensions (JMX) remote API*, JSR 160, November 2006.

[Sun06d] _____, *Java remote method invocation*, <http://java.sun.com/javase/6/docs/platform/rmi/spec/rmiTOC.html>, 2006.

[Sun06e] _____, *Mobile media API (MMAPI) specification, version 1.1*, JSR 135, June 2006.

[Sun08]   _____, *Java management extensions (JMX) specification, version 2.0*, JSR 255, February 2008.

[Sun09a] _____, *Developer resources for Java technology*, <http://java.sun.com/>, 1994-2009.

[Sun09b] _____, *PersonalJava application environment*, <http://java.sun.com/products/personaljava/>, 1994-2009.

[Sun09c] _____, *Metro*, <https://metro.dev.java.net/>, 2009.

[Sun09d] _____, *Trail: The reflection API*, <http://java.sun.com/docs/books/tutorial/reflect/index.html>, 2009.

[SV03]   H. Schulzrinne and B. Volz, *Dynamic host configuration protocol (DHCPv6) options for session initiation protocol (SIP) servers*, IETF RFC 3319, 2003.

[Szy02]   C. Szyperski, *Component software: Beyond object-oriented programming*, 2nd ed., Addison-Wesley Professional, November 2002.

[The07a] The Internet Society, *JXTA v2.0 protocols specification*, Tech. report, Sun Microsystems, October 2007.

[The07b] The JacORB Team, *JacORB 2.3 programming guide*, February 2007.

Bibliography

[TIS08]   TISPAN, *IP multimedia call control protocol based on session initiation protocol (SIP) and session description protocol (SDP)*, TS 24.229 [Release 7], 3GPP, May 2008.

[TK02]   R. Tolksdorf and K. Knubben, *Programming distributed systems with the delegation-based object-oriented language dSelf*, SAC '02: ACM Symposium on Applied Computing, March 2002.

[TST01]   K. Takashio, G. Soeda, and H. Tokuda, *A mobile agent framework for follow-me applications in ubiquitous computing environment*, ICDCSW '01: International Conference on Distributed Computing Systems Workshops, IEEE Computer Society, April 2001.

[VRMCL09] L. M. Vaquero, L. Rodero-Merino, J. Caceres, and M. Lindner, *A break in the clouds: towards a cloud definition*, ACM SIGCOMM Computer Communication Review (CCR) **39** (2009), no. 1, 50–55.

[W3C02]   W3C, *XML encryption syntax and processing*, <http://www.w3.org/TR/xmlenc-core/>, December 2002.

[W3C04a]   _____, *OWL Web ontology language overview*, <http://www.w3.org/TR/owl-features/>, February 2004.

[W3C04b]   _____, *Resource description framework (RDF): Concepts and abstract syntax*, <http://www.w3.org/TR/rdf-concepts/>, February 2004.

[W3C04c]   W3C, *Web services architecture*, <http://www.w3.org/TR/ws-arch/>, February 2004.

[W3C04d]   _____, *XML schema part 2: Datatypes second edition*, <http://www.w3.org/TR/xmlschema-2/>, October 2004.

[W3C07a]   W3C, *Composite capability/preference profiles (CC/PP): Structure and vocabularies 2.0*, <http://www.w3.org/TR/CCPP-struct-vocab2/>, April 2007.

[W3C07b]   _____, *SOAP version 1.2 part 1: Messaging framework*, <http://www.w3.org/TR/soap12-part1/>, April 2007.

[W3C07c]   W3C, *SOAP version 1.2 part 2: Adjuncts (second edition)*, <www.w3.org/TR/soap12-part2/>, April 2007.

[W3C07d]   W3C, *SOAP version 1.2 specification assertions and test collection*, <http://www.w3.org/TR/soap12-testcollection>, April 2007.

Bibliography

[W3C07e] _____, *Web services description language (WSDL) version 2.0 part 1: Core language*, <http://www.w3.org/TR/wsdl20/>, June 2007.

[W3C08] _____, *SPARQL query language for RDF*, <http://www.w3.org/TR/rdf-sparql-query/>, January 2008.

[WBMS07] D. Willis, D. Bryan, P. Matthews, and E. Shim, *Concepts and terminology for peer to peer SIP*, IETF Internet-Draft draft-willis-p2psip-concepts-04, March 2007.

[WBS03] I. Wald, C. Benthin, and P. Slusallek, *Distributed interactive ray tracing of dynamic scenes*, PVG '03: IEEE Symposium on Parallel and Large-Data Visualization and Graphics, IEEE Computer Society, October 2003.

[Wei91] M. Weiser, *The computer for the 21st Century*, Scientific American **265** (1991), no. 3, 66–75.

[WLAG93] R. Wahbe, S. Lucco, T. E. Anderson, and S. L. Graham, *Efficient software-based fault isolation*, SIGOPS Operating Systems Review (OSR) **27** (1993), no. 5, 203–216.

[ZB07] M. Zangrilli and D. Bryan, *A chord-based DHT for resource lookup in P2PSIP*, IETF draft-zangrilli-p2psip-dsip-dhtchord-00, February 2007.

[ZME06] S. Zachariadis, C. Mascolo, and W. Emmerich, *The SATIN component system-a metamodel for engineering adaptable mobile systems*, IEEE Transactions on Software Engineering (TOSE) **32** (2006), no. 11, 910–927.

List of Figures

2.1	Basic workflow of ray tracing application	13
2.2	Basic workflow of mobile multimedia player	14
2.3	Basic workflow of report application	15
3.1	Related approaches: support for heterogeneity, mobility and fundamental adaptivity	25
3.2	Related approaches: support for communication types	26
3.3	AXM facet concept: fundamental adaptation leads to dynamic composition of particular state, functionality, implementation and location while maintaining a unique application identity	28
3.4	AXM supports dynamic fundamental application adaptation with respect to the four orthogonal axes location, functionality, implementation and state at runtime	29
3.5	AXM facet concept: fundamental adaptation from one application facet into another one	31
3.6	Common and facet-dependent interfaces of an AXM application	33
3.7	Collaboration of logical entities for AXM	34
3.8	Collaboration of implementation entities for AOM	38
3.9	Coordination of concurrent invocations in AOM (with pseudo code)	39
3.10	Dynamic loading of code with AOM	41
3.11	Abstract `AOMObjectImpl` class (Java)	43
3.12	Collaboration of implementation entities for AWSM	45
3.13	WSDL description with implementation-independent state	46
3.14	Dynamic loading of code with AWSM	48
3.15	Abstract `AWSMServiceImpl` class (Java)	49
3.16	AXM implementation of a ray tracing application	51
3.17	Evaluation hardware and software	52
3.18	Invocation time at the factory finder and the state store	52
3.19	AOM: Duration of fundamental adaptation of the ray tracing application facets	53

List of Figures

3.20	AWSM: Duration of fundamental adaptation of the ray tracing application facets	55
3.21	Network data volume of fundamental adaptation of the ray tracing application	56
3.22	AWSM implementation of mobile multimedia player application components	57
3.23	AXM implementation of report application	59
3.24	Network data volume of fundamental adaptation of the report application	61
4.1	Performance and memory consumption of OSGi HTTP implementations	67
4.2	Process of automatically loading implementation code	70
4.3	Description of implementation code	70
4.4	Relations of DCM JXTA advertisements	75
4.5	Dynamic code management services	76
4.6	Dynamic code selection process for an HTTP service	77
4.7	Resolve descriptor with IDA dependency	78
4.8	DCM architecture for OSGi	79
4.9	Exemplary code description manifest	80
4.10	Bundle manifest with dependency on HTTPBase bundle	81
4.11	Evaluation of bundle loading time with DCM vs. OBR	83
4.12	Integration of DCM with AWSM	85
4.13	Context model structure	91
4.14	Context service architecture	92
4.15	Context management	93
4.16	Sample context query in SPARQL	94
4.17	`ContextAwareAWSMService` interface (Java)	96
4.18	Context-aware mobile media player GUI	97
4.19	Message flow for SIP session establishment	100
4.20	Standard SIP call setup and termination between Alice and Bob	101
4.21	Entity registration using SIP REGISTER request	102
4.22	REGISTER-request containing SLP service description of a printer service	103
4.23	Entity discovery using SIP OPTIONS request	104
4.24	OPTIONS-request containing SLP query	105
4.25	Message flow for SIP session establishment	109
4.26	Extended advertisement with printer service information	110
4.27	Local area network	112
4.28	Point-to-point network	113
4.29	Wide area network	114
4.30	Number of total packets during simulation according to participating SIP entities in point-to-point network	115

List of Figures

4.31	SoapME architecture	119
4.32	Web service proxy SOAP processing chain	120
4.33	Grammar of local communication format	122
4.34	`Service` interface	124
4.35	Abstract `ServiceObject` class	124
4.36	`Interceptor` interface	125
4.37	Hello World service implementation	125
4.38	Evaluation setup	126
4.39	Evaluation of service invocation duration	127
5.1	MDA-like development of a SAMProc	133
5.2	Basic BPEL process description	135
5.3	Basic SAMPEL process description	136
5.4	Basic SAMPEL scope description	136
5.5	Partner links	137
5.6	Partner link example	138
5.7	Variable description example	139
5.8	Correlation set to identify report instance	140
5.9	SAMPEL: method description for reporter	141
5.10	SAMPEL example for distribution aspects	142
5.11	SAMPEL: invocation at supervisor	142
5.12	SAMPEL: wait for an invocation at the supervisor	143
5.13	SAMPEL: replying to an invocation at the supervisor	143
5.14	SAMPEL: assigning a variable	144
5.15	SAMPEL: explicit wait for one minute	144
5.16	SAMPEL: extensible reporter activity	144
5.17	SAMPEL: fundamental adaptation to reviewer facet	145
5.18	SAMPEL: conditional fundamental adaptation	145
5.19	SAMPEL code generator	146
5.20	SAMPEL code generation: determination of interfaces and respective state	147
5.21	SAMPEL: Java code for an explicit method definition	149
5.22	SAMPEL: Java code for Web service invocation	150
5.23	SAMPEL: Java code for fundamental *AWSM service* adaptation	150
5.24	SAMPEL: Java code example for getter/setter methods accessing local variables	151
5.25	SAMPEL diagram editor with a report application model	153
5.26	SAMPEL editor validation	154

List of Abbreviations

AmOP ambient-oriented programming

AOM adaptive object migration

API application programming interface

ATS Agent Transport Service

AWSM adaptive Web service migration

AXM adaptive x migration

BPEL Business Process Execution Language

BPMN Business Process Modelling Notation

CC/PP Composite Capability/Preference Profiles

CDA code description advertisement

CDC Connected Device Configuration

CDR Common Data Representation

CLDC Connected Limited Device Configuration

CORBA Common Object Request Broker Architecture

DCM dynamic code management

DEMAC Distributed Environment for Mobility-aware Computing

DHCP Dynamic Host Configuration Protocol

DLS Dynamic Loading Service

DNS Domain Name System

List of Abbreviations

EBNF Extended Backus-Naur Form

EMF Eclipse Modeling Framework

FROB frugal object

GMF Graphical Modeling Framework

GUI graphical user interface

HTTP Hypertext Transfer Protocol

IDA interface description advertisement

IDL Interface Definition Language

IETF Internet Engineering Task Force

IMS IP Multimedia Subsystem

IP Internet Protocol

JAXB Java Architecture for XML Binding

JMF Java Media Framework

JMX Java Management Extensions

JVM Java Virtual Machine

JXTA-LOC JXTA-based SIP location service

KVM Kilobyte VM

LAN local area network

LCS Life Cycle Service

MA mobile agent

MADAM Mobility and Adaptation Enabling Middleware

MASC Manageable and Adaptive Service Compositions

MDA model-driven architecture

MDD model-driven development

ME Micro Edition

MIDP Mobile Information Device Profile

MMAPI Mobile Media API

MVC Model-View-Controller

oAW-Check openArchitectureWare Check

OBR OSGi Bundle Repository

OMG Object Management Group

ORB Object Request Broker

ORM Object Role Modelling

OTA over-the-air

OWL Web Ontology Language

P2P peer-to-peer

PC personal computer

PDA personal digital assistant

PKI public key infrastructure

POA Portable Object Adapter

PTP point-to-point network

RA resource advertisement

RDF Resource Description Framework

SAMPEL Self-adaptive Mobile Process Execution Language

SAMProc self-adaptive mobile process

SDP Session Description Protocol

SIP Session Initiation Protocol

SLP Service Location Protocol

SOA service-oriented architecture

SOMA Secure and Open Mobile Agent

List of Abbreviations

SPARQL SPARQL Protocol and RDF Query Language

SSL Secure Sockets Layer

SWT Standard Widget Toolkit

TCP Transmission Control Protocol

UA user agent

UbiComp ubiquitous computing

UDDI Universal Description, Discovery and Integration

UDP User Datagram Protocol

URI Uniform Resource Identifier

URL Uniform Resource Location

UUID Universally Unique Identifier

VM virtual machine

VoD Video on Demand

VoIP Voice over IP

WAN wide area network

WSDL Web Services Description Language

Die VDM Verlagsservicegesellschaft sucht für wissenschaftliche Verlage abgeschlossene und herausragende

Dissertationen, Habilitationen, Diplomarbeiten, Master Theses, Magisterarbeiten usw.

für die kostenlose Publikation als Fachbuch.

Sie verfügen über eine Arbeit, die hohen inhaltlichen und formalen Ansprüchen genügt, und haben Interesse an einer honorarvergüteten Publikation?

Dann senden Sie bitte erste Informationen über sich und Ihre Arbeit per Email an *info@vdm-vsg.de*.

Sie erhalten kurzfristig unser Feedback!

VDM Verlagsservicegesellschaft mbH
Dudweiler Landstr. 99
D - 66123 Saarbrücken

Telefon +49 681 3720 174
Fax +49 681 3720 1749

www.vdm-vsg.de

Die VDM Verlagsservicegesellschaft mbH vertritt

MIX
Papier aus verantwortungsvollen Quellen
Paper from responsible sources
FSC® C105338

Printed by Books on Demand GmbH, Norderstedt / Germany